GENERAL PITT-RIVERS

Pitt-Rivers in his early fifties

GENERAL PITT-RIVERS

Evolution and Archaeology in the Nineteenth Century

BY
M. W. THOMPSON

MOONRAKER PRESS

First published in 1977 by Moonraker Press
26 St Margaret's Street, Bradford-on-Avon, Wiltshire

SBN 239.00162.1

Text set in 11 pt Photon Times, printed by
photolithography, and bound in Great Britain
at The Pitman Press, Bath

CONTENTS

LIST OF ILLUSTRATIONS

PREFACE

Among those who know the name of Pitt-Rivers there are some who find the man and his activities repellent and others who set him on a pedestal as one who did no wrong, a genius whom we must venerate. The present author first met the name of Pitt-Rivers as an archaeology student at Cambridge and his reaction was certainly to go into the former of these two categories. The rather gloomy museums at Oxford and Farnham, Dorset, combined with the intensely serious nature of the General's pronouncements, were not calculated to arouse the enthusiasm of an undergraduate.

A few years later at the Ministry of Works I came across 16 notebooks and sketch-books Pitt-Rivers used on his journeys as Inspector, written by himself and his assistants, which had been given to the Ministry in the 1920s. During the course of their study I spent a day as a guest with the late H. St George Gray and his wife at their charming medieval house at Martock, Somerset and I also enjoyed the kind hospitality of the late Captain George Pitt-Rivers, the General's grandson, at Hinton St Mary. After the publication of an article on this it seemed unlikely that I should encounter Pitt-Rivers again. Some 14 years later as a result of various circumstances I found myself privileged to catalogue the collection of Pitt-Rivers papers acquired by the Salisbury and South Wiltshire Museum. So my thoughts inevitably turned to a biography.

My own official duties in Wales have precluded the possibility of an exhaustive or definitive work, a project indeed towards which I was not attracted and to which in any case the available material does not easily lend itself. I have also avoided any attempt to cover more than superficially the studies of Pitt-Rivers on material culture or his excavations, which would have required a work of quite a different format and character, and I may add quite a different kind of author. What then does this essay—and I use the word advisedly—set out to do?

As I have said, Pitt-Rivers has tended to be regarded either as a figure of fun, so shrouded in seriosity as not to be taken seriously, or quite the reverse, as a self-evident genius whom it would be sacrilegious to criticize. For the historian or biographer neither of these attitudes is enough; what he seeks is two things, what did Pitt-Rivers do and why

7

did he do it? Motivation is elusive enough in living persons and indeed in oneself but in a person long dead it is of course that much more difficult to identify. Yet this is the task that the biographer must always set himself, for without some understanding of motivation a man's actions become meaningless. Of no one can this be more truly said than of Pitt-Rivers. Once we can enter into the intensely serious habits of thought to which his mind was attuned many things become intelligible.

These then have been my objectives, first to ascertain the facts of the life of Pitt-Rivers—not always an easy matter; and second, from these, taking into account the nineteenth-century background in which he worked, to try to make an intelligible narrative of his activities. The difficulties are considerable partly due to ignorance about his life and still more his personality (there are no diaries and few autograph letters), and partly because Pitt-Rivers himself tended in later years to give, sometimes merely by silence, a misleading picture of his earlier life. For example his professional career began in Ireland while he was stationed at Cork although his silence on the subject in later life would hardly have led one to realize this. More serious perhaps is the picture that Pitt-Rivers tended to present of himself as a man like Spencer who knew all about evolution before the publication of the *Origin of Species*. This is to confuse progress with Darwinian evolution, for it was the realization, probably as a sort of revelation in the early 1860s, of the analogy between his typological series and the biological evolution of Darwin that converted Pitt-Rivers from a collector to a scientist, into a man with a mission to unveil the laws of cultural evolution.

After tracing his early military career I have followed the three interests of his professional life: cultural evolution, fieldwork and protection of monuments. In the concluding chapters on Cranborne Chase I have dealt cursorily with the excavations which have been so ably reinterpreted for us by Professor Hawkes. The personal accounts have allowed a more detailed treatment of the organisation and background to work in the field which have a special interest in view of the great expansion of archaeological work at the present time. It must be a very sobering thought that the whole of the excavation programme in Cranborne Chase cost a fraction of what it costs now to maintain a University Archaeology Department for a year.

A word is necessary about sources. The difficulty of the biographer of Pitt-Rivers is the scarcity of autograph letters and absence of diaries which are so valuable as a key to personality. The Salisbury collection which contains about 4,000 letters received (normally without replies) is the most important collection, containing also valuable material on the Inspectorship and all aspects of his professional work. The Public Record Office holds the 16 notebooks and sketch-books already mentioned while the Dorset County Record Office has two large volumes of autograph personal accounts of which I have made extensive use in my last two chapters. Early material is to be found in the Lane Fox papers in the Leeds City Archive, and Mr Anthony Pitt-Rivers has most courteously allowed me to look at the letters (mainly early) in his possession, although at the time of writing I had not had an opportunity to study them in detail.

Among printed material the memoir of the late St George Gray is chiefly valuable for its complete list of the 100-odd published works of the General. For the second half of his life the professional publications of Pitt-Rivers himself form the essential framework. His main lectures on material culture between 1867–75 were gathered together and published under the title *Cultural Evolution*, unfortunately not in the order in which they were given. Surprisingly there is printed material from his early life in the two volumes of Alderley letters edited by Nancy Mitford, which give valuable details about his courtship, marriage and early married life. Hamilton had first-hand knowledge of Fox in the period 1852–62 and the third volume of his *History of the Grenadier Guards* is an invaluable source. Russell, the *Times* correspondent in the Crimea, probably met Fox in Malta and accompanied the staff of the 2nd Division, in which Fox was serving, from Bulgaria to the landing at the Old Fort and indeed as far as the Alma. He therefore saw the opening part of the campaign from much the same viewpoint as Fox, whom indeed he does mention. Not many biographers are fortunate enough to have had the *Times* correspondent accompany their subject into the Crimea.

I have concluded the book with two appendixes: the first is an unpublished account by Pitt-Rivers of the Battle of the Alma; the second a reprint of his classic lecture *The Evolution of Culture,* the culmination of his series of lectures on material culture. Many of those who know of Pitt-Rivers only through the Cranborne Chase volumes entirely misunderstand his real motivation until they have read this.

While working on the biography I had used a loose-leaf book with a page for each year of the subject's life to get the chronological sequence clear in my own head. From this I developed the chronological table at the end of the book which may be helpful for reference. Nothing indeed has impressed itself more on this biographer's mind than the necessity for attention to chronology; an opinion that Pitt-Rivers held in 1870 might be quite contrary to what he thought in 1880.

The names are confusing and it is important to sort them out before we start. The baptismal registers of the children of Pitt-Rivers show that Lane was treated as a Christian name, not part of the surname. From 1827–80 the correct name of Pitt-Rivers was Augustus Henry Lane Fox (without a hyphen). He is indexed under Fox in Army Lists and in the Alderley letters his wife's relatives always call him Fox. I normally refer to him as Fox when speaking of events before 1880.

Under the terms of the will of Lord Rivers he was obliged to take the additional surname of Pitt-Rivers, thus A.H.L.F. Pitt-Rivers, while his children had to take the additional name of Pitt, thus A. E. L. Fox-Pitt. Just occasionally one finds Fox-Pitt-Rivers which was strictly speaking permissible. In signatures and on the title pages of the Cranborne Chase volumes Pitt-Rivers did not use a hyphen, thus Lieutenant-General Pitt Rivers. The hyphen is therefore optional but as it is normal now to do so I have used one throughout this book.

M. W. THOMPSON
CARDIFF, January 1976

I
CHILDHOOD AND BOYHOOD

Augustus Henry Lane Fox, who later added Pitt-Rivers to his surname, was born on 14 April 1827 at Hope Hall, just outside the northern edge of the park of Bramham Park which adjoins the Great North Road a few miles south of Wetherby in the West Riding of Yorkshire. A rambling eighteenth-century building, now inhabited by trainees of the adjoining racing stables, in the nineteenth century it was variously let as a shooting lodge or occupied by younger brothers or older relatives of the head of the Lane Fox family, whose seat was in the mansion of Bramham Park.

The mansion itself, a fine early eighteenth-century building, together with the formal gardens, had been erected by Robert Benson first Lord Bingley, possibly to his own design, in the reign of Queen Anne. His daughter and heiress, Harriet, married George Fox to whom she brought the property. Fox had also inherited a vast estate from his mother, Frances Lane before her marriage, daughter of Sir George Lane of Tulske, and by Act of Parliament in 1751 had assumed the surname and arms of Lane. George Fox Lane died without direct heir in 1773 and was succeeded by his nephew James Fox Lane.[1] He married in 1789 Marcia Lucy Pitt, youngest daughter of George Lord Rivers—the fateful marriage from which stemmed in due course the inheritance of the Cranborne Chase estate by the subject of our essay. There were four sons and one daughter of this marriage. At the time in question (1827) the eldest son George Lane Fox (Fox and Lane were reversed in this generation), who had inherited the property in 1821, was living in the great house, while his younger brother, William Augustus Lane Fox, the father of Augustus, was living outside the park but still on estate property at Hope Hall.

About William Augustus Lane Fox we have very little information except that he was born in 1795, was commissioned as an Ensign in the Grenadier Guards in January 1811 and became Lieutenant and Captain in December 1813.[2] He saw active service in Spain and in September 1818 exchanged to the 98th Foot (the North Staffordshire Regiment), no doubt to be nearer home. In December 1817 he married Lady Caroline Douglas who bore him two sons, William Edward born in 1818 and Augustus Henry (born in 1827) whom we met in the first

11

paragraph. Augustus was then the younger of two brothers between whom there was a considerable gap in age, nine years. Born in Yorkshire as if a presage of future events he was christened in Dorset by his uncle, the incumbent of Sturminster Newton.[2a]

Lady Caroline Fox, the mother of Augustus, outlived her husband by 40 or more years and as the responsibility for the upbringing of her younger son largely fell upon her, she was undoubtedly the parent who had more influence on him. We know little about her except her pedigree which is a distinguished one. Caroline Douglas was a Scottish aristocrat, descended from James, 14th Earl of Morton (1703–68), whose grandson, John, married Lady Frances Lascelles. She bore him four sons and six daughters of whom Caroline was the youngest. Her eldest brother was George Sholto, 18th Earl of Morton and through the marriages of her other brothers and sisters she was connected with many of the leading Scottish families. Although always referred to as Lady Caroline Fox, whether the title was properly used is not clear.

From this background three points are clear. Augustus Lane Fox was born into the landed, aristocratic level of society. Nevertheless he was the younger son of a younger son with slight expectations, of which he must have been very conscious in early life. Thirdly, some aspects of his character—earnestness, pragmatism, determination—are much more intelligible in the son of a Yorkshire father and a Scottish mother.

On 29 July 1828 the mansion at Bramham Park went up in flames, or rather the roof did, for the walls remained standing. George Lane Fox's finances did not permit him to repair the building which remained a roofless shell until the early years of the present century, but the gardens and grounds were maintained. It was in this curious condition that Augustus must have known the park (the family had moved from Hope Hall to Bramham Biggin, a fine seventeenth-century house by the park entry).[3] It can be supposed that recollections of the grounds at Bramham Park, more particularly the Black Fen Pleasure Grounds, were the initial inspiration for the Larmer Grounds that Pitt-Rivers himself laid out when he had come into the great inheritance of the Rivers estates. He started by erecting a circular temple recalling the Ionic temple at Bramham Park while the wooded setting and the relationship of grounds to mansion at the Larmer Grounds at once recall Bramham (**2**).

William Augustus Lane Fox died at Torquay on 11 February 1832 at the age of 36. The tablet on the south wall of the chancel of Bramham church records:

Though he walked through the valley of the Shadow of Death; he feared no evil for the Lord was his light and his salvation. For the Dead there are many mourners, but only one monument, the bosom which loved them best.

His elder son, William Edward, also died in his thirties, and although the

2 The Temple at Bramham Park

circumstances of death are not recorded in either case, it is probably reasonable to infer that tuberculosis was the cause of death in both cases.

For Lady Caroline the death of her husband meant that she no longer had a Yorkshire home, or possibly she had no inclination to stay. At all events we find her setting up house at 3 St James's Square soon afterwards. At a very tender age Augustus left his native Yorkshire to move to the capital and although no doubt he paid visits to his relatives, apart from absences on military service he was resident in London for about the next 50 years.

The education of the two boys took very different courses. Of William's school education we have no record but he matriculated on 18 March 1836 at Balliol College, Oxford and in his will dated 23 July 1840 he is described as 'of Baliol College in the University of Oxford.'[4] The fact that he made a will at the tender age of 22 suggests that his health was precarious. He entered the Diplomatic Corps and became an attaché at Berlin and subsequently in Naples.

He died at La Cava on 13 June 1852 while he was an attaché to the British Mission in Naples,[5] at the age of 34.

It was evidently considered that Augustus as a younger son should follow in his father's footsteps and make the army his career. Accordingly it was decided to send him to the Royal Military College at Sandhurst.

At this period Sandhurst differed from today's Academy in two important respects.[6] First, it provided a full secondary education for boys entering at 13, and second all the cadets were fee-paying. 75 of the 180 places were reserved for sons of Officers who paid a reduced fee, the other 105 places being for 'sons of private gentlemen' each of whom paid the full annual fee of £125. It therefore much more resembled a normal public school of the period. However it differed entirely from these in its curriculum which was extremely vocational. To complete the course and obtain a commission without purchase a cadet had to pass examinations, held in public before a board of general officers, in six out of eleven subjects: mathematics (four divisions), fortification (two divisions), military surveying, French, German, History and Latin. One division of mathematics, one of fortification and surveying were compulsory. The cadet was required to have a plane table and compass, mathematical instruments, specialist books on surveying and fortification and so on. A 'Very handsomely fitted Model room' contained a wide range of models on military subjects. The six steps as they were called followed a probationary period in mathematics. Two of the staff taught military sketching to which great importance was attached.

Lane Fox's career at Sandhurst was not a success as the entry in the Register of Gentlemen Cadets of the Royal Military College at Sandhurst records:[7]

FOX, Augustus Henry Lane. Date of admission, 19 Jan. 1841; Age 13 yrs. 9 months; Size: 5′ 6″; Parentage: Private Gentleman (The Lady Caroline Fox, 3 St. James's Square, London); Entered Upper 1st. Arithmetic and Mathematics Class 29 Mar. 1841; Date of retiring: 22 July 1841; Commissioned into Grenadier Guards. Withdrawn by his friends 16 May 1845. Adjutant General's Dept. 1854. By purchase.

The precise meaning of the entry is not clear but it seems to leave no doubt that he spent only six months at the College—between January and July 1841. During the next four years it is not certain how he spent his time although it is fair to assume that he underwent a course of private study that followed more or less along the lines he would have pursued had he stayed at Sandhurst.

It is unfortunate that we have no information about this period because the training he received then was almost certainly the basis of much of his later field techniques. The sketching used in the Inspector's notebooks and his insistence on his assistants' skill in this, the surveying and the ability to use survey instruments, the sectional drawing and ability to record three-dimensionally, the models at Farnham Museum all point to training of the Sandhurst type undertaken during this period. They were skills above that of an ordinary infantry officer, albeit not equal to an artilleryman or engineer who had undergone the highly specialised training at Woolwich.

The Army Lists of the nineteenth century show that the cost of purchase of a commission was related to two factors: (a) the rank of entry and (b) the branch of the Army (infantry, cavalry, horseguards or footguards). Lane Fox was commissioned into the footguards, the Grenadier Guards, on 16 May 1845, as a Lieutenant.

MUSKETRY AND MARRIAGE

The monthly return for June, 1845, marks Lt. Lane Fox as on leave, but in July he is recorded as present.[1] The Grenadier Guards at this period consisted of a body of about 2,400 men divided into three battalions, each battalion forming an autonomous unit.[2] A battalion served six months in a London station as they came round in rotation on March 1 and September 1. Fox was assigned to the third battalion which he joined at Portman Street, then in September he went to St George's, Knightsbridge, then in 1846 Windsor and the Tower, in 1847 to Winchester (the summer rest station) and Portman St., and so on. So far as we know the duties were only ceremonial, although occasionally troops were called upon to assist the Civil power. Thus at the time of the Chartist gatherings in 1848 all three battalions were on stand-by duty, although happily their services were not required.

Relief from this somewhat tedious round of duty came to Captain Lane Fox (he was promoted in 1850) in an unexpected way to which we must now turn our attention.

Except for a small section (The Rifle Brigade) the British army of this period was armed with smooth-bore muskets. It was known that rifling the barrel (making a spiral groove along it) caused the bullet to rotate and greatly improved the precision of the weapon, rather on the same principle as the feathering on an arrow. Rifles had been known since the seventeenth century and were used as sporting guns. Why then had they not been introduced before? The answer lay in the method of loading: the spiralling groove in the barrel could delay or jam the bullet when it was being rammed down the muzzle and all the military small-arms of the period were muzzle-loaded. With a sporting gun this was perhaps not serious but with a military weapon it was quite intolerable. Attempts in France to introduce rifles had been most discouraging and they had been withdrawn.[3]

Experiments had been going on in France for the past two decades in order to overcome this difficulty. Delvigne had invented the expanding bullet; it fitted easily into the barrel on entry, where it rested on a ledge above the charge and the lead was expanded by hammering the ramrod from the top. Subsequently the bullet was given a concave base which the force of the explosion of the charge opened up and caused it to press firmly into the grooves on the way out. With slight modifications introduced by Minié this was the famous Minié rifle of the 1850s. The Government knew of course of the French successes and prompted by this had decided to carry out tests of their own, ostensibly at first to replace the rifles used by the Rifle Brigade. Tests started at Woolwich in 1850 and in 1851 the pattern 51 (the Minié) was selected from the weapons tested. By this time the purpose was to re-arm not merely the Rifle Brigade but the whole army. This proved to be a lengthy process taking several years, by which time the P.51 had been replaced by the P.53 (the Enfield).

A detachment of Grenadier Guards carried out the tests and this is how Fox became involved. The tests in 1850 and 1851 had been under the charge of Major Brownrigg and it is not quite clear when Fox started testing. It is important to remember that Fox himself played no part in the technical improvements of the weapon. He started with testing and this remained one of his duties, but his particular contribution was drill instruction in how to use the new arm. The rifle was loaded in the same way as the smooth bore and for this reason had the same rate of fire as any muzzle-loader, two or three rounds a minute. The smooth-bore had little accuracy over 100 yds and was used, as at Waterloo, for firing at solid bodies of cavalry or infantry at close quarters. The rifle had accuracy up to perhaps 600 yds provided the marksmen knew how to use it: that is to say, could estimate the distance of the target and so adjust the sights correctly, allow for wind and movement of the target, and so on.

... the Army owes much of the theory of the present (1874) system of musketry instruction to Capt. Aug. Lane Fox, of the Grenadier Guards. This officer, who had been employed in the experiments at Woolwich, which led to the introduction of the Minié musket, was appointed, in 1852, to instruct the Second Battalion Grenadier Guards. ... After spending some months on the continent in studying the systems of instruction prevailing in France, Belgium and Piedmont Captain Fox on his return drew up a code comprising aiming, position, judging distance, and other preliminary drills. ... Towards the end of the year, Lord Hardinge (C-in-C), being informed of the steps taken by Captain Fox in the Guards, sent for that officer, discussed with him the project of establishing a Central School for carrying out the same system throughout the service, and desired him to revise his Regulations, so as to make them applicable for general purposes. This he did, and gave his new code the title of *Instruction of Musketry.* ...

... In the following April Lord Hardinge sent Captain Fox to Portsmouth, desiring him to submit his proposed regulations to Colonel Hay, 19th Regiment, who was to be appointed Commandant of the new School of Musketry to be established at Hythe, and after giving six months' instruction to the detachment of various regiments, Captain Fox, with the additional experience he had thus gained, carefully reconsidered and revised the whole code. It was approved by Lord Hardinge, and a first edition was printed and issued,

3 Hythe School of Musketry

appearing necessarily under the authority and name of the Commandant, Colonel Hay. Subsequent revisions were also made by Captain Fox and although certain modifications have from time to time been adopted since that period, the principle remains as originally introduced by him.[4]

Hamilton was a senior officer in the Grenadiers at this time and so he wrote from first-hand knowledge of the events. This is important evidence since Fox later quarrelled fiercely with Hay who accordingly tended to minimise his part in setting up the School. In the first three Annual Reports of the School there is no reference to Fox except indirectly in severe criticism of the training in Malta (where Fox was in charge).

Before the army acquired the heathland areas of Hampshire and Surrey for training purposes during the Crimean War, when new accommodation was required it was usual to re-vitalize buildings of the Napoleonic era. Such was the case with the School of Musketry when two handsome early nineteenth-century blocks that formed part of the defences against French invasion were brought into use (**3**). The wide dunes of the foreshore were utilized for the ranges; a 2,000-yd range for testing and several 600-yd ranges for training.

Fox and his wife came into residence in the summer of 1853 and we know that their first child (still-born) was born in the building in November.[5] He was concerned with testing the Enfield and Lancaster rifles, for parties only started arriving for instruction after he had left for the Mediterranean early in the new year (after only some six months at the school).

The first edition of *Instruction of Musketry*, a slim red manual measuring 8 × 3 in. appeared just about the time Fox went overseas. It is an impressive work for its 26-year-old author, whose authorship is revealed on page 34 when he uses his own initials to illustrate a marked erasure. It explained the system of training to be used at Hythe and three copies were sent to every depot. The instruction comprised: theory (trajectory of the bullet), practice drill (cleaning, target, judging distance and manufacture of cartridges), practice (target and judging distance). In the latter case there was a system of selection into three grades of proficiency. In one memorable phrase the author betrays his own interests (p. 8):

... the instructor, after having thoroughly explained the principles contained in this book, will be at liberty to advance deeper into the subject, developing, to a degree proportional to the rank and intelligence of his auditors, the whole history of firearms. ...

We have now to retrace our steps and speak of his marriage to Alice Margaret Stanley at St George's Church, Hanover Square, on 2 February 1853.[5a] The letters between her grandmother and mother and father that were edited by Nancy Mitford in the 1930s provide a good deal of information about the courtship and early years of marriage. The Editor suppressed some letters as too revealing and those that were published are sometimes embarrassing.

Alice 'came out' on 5 February 1846.[6] The ladies made determined efforts to find her a husband but without success. In May, 1850: 'I do wish Alice had a good husband of some kind or other, she could do so well with a child every year I have no doubt.'[7] Fox probably met her about 1848 for his first proposal of marriage in 1849 was rebuffed, not by Alice but by her parents on the grounds of his lack of prospects. He persisted: '... the young Major and Alice laughed at each other's jokes ...' (4.9.1851).[8] The death of Augustus's elder brother transformed his prospects since he was now the only son and heir.[9] His mother was expected to leave him £25,000 and in addition he had his commission. After a good deal of acrimony the marriage took place.

The partnership which lasted 47 years, albeit founded on affection, was a stormy one. Fox was of a moody and irascible disposition or at any rate so we may infer from Kate Stanley's accounts of the treatment of his wife.[10] Alice was not free from fault and a meanness or stinginess of character remarked by her mother stayed with her for the rest of her life. The economies practised at Rushmore were notorious in later years. We may wonder indeed if some of the privations of early marriage were not self-inflicted. At all events whatever the short-comings of the marriage it was a fruitful one and apart from the still-born child in 1853 nine children who reached adulthood were born to the couple between 1855 and 1866.

The Stanleys of Alderley in Cheshire were a remarkable family. The first Lord Stanley (1766–1850) had been a considerable scholar, while his wife, Lady Maria-Josepha (1771–1863) had been in France during the Revolution, knew Gibbon and in the 1840s and '50s entertained Carlyle and John Stuart Mill at Alderley. In London there were literary dinners at her house. Lord Edward John Stanley, who succeeded to the title in 1850, was a conservative politician who held office as President of the Board of Trade and Postmaster-General, and leading politicians were entertained at the house. He was in a position to have influenced Fox's military career and almost certainly did so. He was known as 'Benjamin Backbite' at Westminster and the letters, although often amusing, leave little doubt that the nickname was well earned. His wife, Lady Henrietta-Maria Stanley, was a formidable personality, a feminist who had lived abroad much in her youth. Unfortunately Alice was not a favourite child and the letters between these three about her and Fox are usually scathing.

More important for Fox was the influence of his own age group, the three brothers and five sisters of Alice. They were all exceptionally gifted, although the eldest son who became an Arabist and a Mohameddan (to the consternation of the family) must be regarded as eccentric. He was the main member of the family to support the stormy romance between Fox and Alice. Bertrand Russell, who knew the family later in the century, described them thus: 'The Stanleys were a large family of exceptional vigour, healthy, boisterous, argumentative, each with his or her own very definite opinions on religion and politics, and each disagreeing with all the others.'[11]

The Bramham background of Fox was a sporting one, alien to pursuits of the mind, so there can be little doubt that the Stanleys had an extremely stimulating intellectual influence on him. Kate Stanley wrote on 2 February 1961:

Augustus is very full of Plato just now and likes it so much, also of a book on education by Bray which he gives me to read and I did so. It is rather on the phrenology system. . . . I never knew anyone put his ideas and principles so little into practice as Augustus. . . .[12]

It was not of course only the Stanleys who influenced the intellectual development of Fox but also the friends that he met at their house. Alice's name had been associated in 1846 with young Egerton, the son of Sir Philip de Malpas Grey-Egerton (1806–81). Like Lord Edward Stanley he had been at Christ Church, while he was the member for S. Cheshire when Stanley was the member for N. Cheshire. After leaving Oxford he had started a collection of fossil fish on which he became an authority although he published historical as well as scientific works. He was of a kindly and genial disposition and we may suspect that he played some part in Fox's decision to form his own collection of weapons.[13]

Another person whom Fox must have met was Albert Way (1805–74), who was Director of the Society of Antiquaries 1842–46 and a founder of the Archaeological Institute in 1845; he had married Emmeline Stanley, Alice's aunt, in 1844. Although he was interested in later periods he was a skilled draughtsman. He was one of Fox's sponsors for Fellowship of the Society of Antiquaries in 1863.

It was against this background that Fox began his collection, the collection in which it was not so much the objects as their arrangement by sequence of forms (typology was the word invented by Fox himself in later years, *see* p. 41) that made it unusual. It should be said at once that we have no reliable information on when he started it nor what it consisted of in the first ten years. No records survive from the period and the collection had been transformed so much before it was given to Oxford University (let alone since) that there is no trustworthy information about its extent or arrangement in the 1850s. The incomplete catalogue of 1874 and 1877 only tells us of the collection at that date and in any case is in some ways more of a manual than a catalogue. Another extremely important point to remember is that Fox profoundly modified his views after 1860 in conformity with Darwinian ideas, and remarks that he made after that date were almost certainly coloured by this. As Fox tended to portray himself as a man, like Spencer, who had discovered evolution before the publication of the *Origin* there is even more reason to exercise caution.

From chance remarks by Fox at a later date it seems clear he was involved in the testing at Woolwich by 1851 and had started collecting by 1852. There are hints in *Instructions of Musketry* written at this time that he had become fairly involved in the history of firearms (p. 18). The collection probably started with muskets and extended to other firearms, weapons and primitive weapons. The collections of the United Service Institution and Henry Christy were probably major factors in the later extensions but we have no evidence for chronology.

As he was testing at Woolwich he was concerned principally with failures, since the army could adopt only one weapon for its use. In his excellent lecture on the Rifle in 1858 he tells us that he would be concerned only with the main 'links in the chain of progress' ignoring those side branches which contributed nothing 'however ingenious in themselves'. It is probably fair to assume that this was the basis of the arrangement of his own collection. Beyond this it is unwise to speculate.

There is an interesting analogy with Henry Christy (1810–64). Fox's collection was profoundly influenced by that of Christy at a later date, as he recognized.[14] Christy, a banker, started travelling in 1850 in foreign countries to study their characteristics and in 1851 'The Great

Exhibition' powerfully influenced his mind, and he began the study of the primitive habits and customs of uncivilized tribes.[15] In 1852–3 he travelled in Scandinavia where he became interested in their prehistoric collections.

Fox almost certainly had no interest in prehistoric things at this early date although he followed a very similar path of development in later times. The Great Exhibition produced a strong consciousness of material progress and a theory which sought to elucidate this apparently relentless progress—as did the series of Fox—had a decided relevance to the contemporary world. He arranged his weapons or muskets in a series showing a system, the gradual improvement and development of the form, which could of course be extended to all branches of material culture. It demonstrated the underlying principles of material progress of which the culmination in many fields was to be seen in the Crystal Palace.

III
OVERSEAS SERVICE

In the summer of 1853 there were considerable military exercises near Chobham, Surrey, an unheard of event for the army of that period. It was an indication that a war atmosphere was building up. Troops began embarkation for the Mediterranean early in the following year. The 3rd Battalion of the Grenadier Guards to which Fox had formerly belonged marched from St George's Barracks to Waterloo on 22 February to take the train for Southampton, where they embarked on the *Ripon* and *Manilla*. They disembarked at Malta on 5 March 1854.

Captain Fox (the title of Major accorded him in the Stanley letters was the courtesy extended to Guards officers of always using the rank higher than they held) had possibly travelled earlier although he may have accompanied them. Hamilton (an eye-witness) described his position thus:

Owing to this recent introduction of a new arm, the Battalions of Guards, during their stay at Malta, were frequently exercised at the target, according to the new regulations, under the superintendence of Captain Fox, who had been sent out by Lord Hardinge to Malta 'on particular service' to instruct the regiments in its use, whatever their destination. That officer was eventually to form if possible a school of musketry with the army in the field ... the sites chosen for practice were St George's and St Julian's Bays, Slena, Fort Tigue and others.[1]

W. H. Russell, the *Times* correspondent, whose dispatches to his paper achieved such fame, had travelled on the *Ripon* and he took a keen interest in the rifle practice and drill. The method of teaching the judgement of distances was described for *Times* readers in some detail.[2] Fox knew Russell later on and it is likely that they first met in Malta.

Fox spent about six weeks or so training and testing on the coastal dunes of Malta. He was still testing the Enfield and Lancaster.[3] The former had already been chosen as the army weapon, although the greatly improved performance of the Lancaster then and later made some doubt the wisdom of this decision.

Malta was a staging post for English and French troops before going on to Turkey. Fox sailed with the Grenadiers in the *Golden Fleece* on 22 April[4] and disembarked at Scutari. The battalions of regimental troops, virtually one from each regiment, were formed into brigades with two of these in each case in the five divisions. The Turks were engaged in fighting the Russians on the Danube and understandably felt that their Allies, rather than defending Constantinople (not yet necessary) should engage the enemy on this front. The Allied army therefore moved over in stages in mid-June to Varna on the Bulgarian coast of the Black Sea.

'As the school of musketry was for a time partially suspended, on leaving Scutari, Captain Augustus Fox accepted the post of Deputy Assistant Quarter Master General, and though occasionally occupied with his duties as Musketry Instructor, he accompanied Sir De Lacy Evans to the Crimea. . . .'[5]

The army spent nearly three months under canvas in Bulgaria. Cholera broke out in mid-July causing many deaths and a great deal of despondency. Even those not afflicted by cholera suffered from various stomach troubles. How Fox fared is not known, but we do know that his immediate superior, the Assistant Q.M., was so ill that Fox had to stand in for him as he did later when he was wounded at the Alma.[5a]

As the Russian army had retreated from the Danube the Allied commanders were in something of a dilemma as to what to do next, although both Home Governments were determined to make Sevastopol the objective of the expedition. The momentous decision was taken in the late Summer and the troops embarked in the second week of September. This time the ships did not travel individually but in one vast armada. Practically the whole army landed at the Old Fort on the dunes about 20 miles north of Sevastopol on 14 September. Of this extraordinary operation we can only echo the words of Russell '. . . not bold simply. It was rash. Boldness may be justified.'[6]

Fox travelled in the *City of London* together with De Lacy Evans's staff and the 41st (the Welch Regiment). Russell was invited to accompany them and he more or less attached himself to the 2nd Division staff for the next few days after the landing. He must therefore have got to know Fox quite well.

On the nineteenth the two Allied armies (for they were under separate command) were ready to march south towards Sevastopol. As the country was open without obstacles of any kind the two armies were able to march in full formation, the French (who had no cavalry) together with 9,000 Turks on the seaward side, and the English on the landward side. The French were fairly soberly attired, but in the English army every regiment was in full uniform with an astonishing display of colours and hats. Fox was the only Guardsman in the 2nd Division and presumably wore bearskin and full uniform. As a Staff officer, albeit a very junior one, he was no doubt mounted.

The Russians had taken up a position on the south side of the river Alma, a stream flowing west into the Black Sea, which was spanned by a bridge carrying the road to Sevastopol. The battle of the Alma took place on 20 September when the Allied armies moved forward to storm the Russian positions. The French on the seaward side had covering fire from Allied warships but they had to scale some formidable heights in order to reach the level ground where the Russians were stationed. With the French part we are not here concerned and with the English only in so far as it affected the subject of our essay.

The English army led by the Light Division and the 2nd Division, both in line, the former on the left and the latter on the right, advanced until they were in view of the Russians. The plan was for the English to wait for the French to advance on the right under cover from the Allied warships. The army had the galling experience of having to lie in their uncomfortable uniforms on the ground. About midday Lord Raglan gave the order 'The Infantry will advance'. To the sound of bugles 10,000 men got to their feet and dressed themselves into one enormous line, over a mile long and two men deep.

It was a point of honour among the mounted staff officers that to encourage the men they should expose themselves to the maximum. Lord Raglan set an example by making a private sortie into the enemy lines and establishing a look-out post on the hill behind them. Fox as a very junior staff officer was probably mainly concerned with taking messages. Communication was a difficult problem as the charge of the Light Brigade was later to show.

The south bank of the Alma was precipitous and so provided dead ground concealed from enemy fire. The brigade on the left of the Light Division was unable to mount the slope but Codrington's Brigade on the right climbed the bank and in a confused mass charged up the hill towards the redoubt. The redoubt was a Russian gun emplacement and their guns firing point blank at Codrington's Brigade took a heavy toll. However they were forced to withdraw their guns and the redoubt was taken. Russian reinforcements now arrived and after some wavering Codrington's Brigade retreated down the hill again. The 1st Division, including the Guards battalions, had now crossed the river and this was the turning point of the battle. They moved up the hill and allowed Codrington's Brigade to reform.

The 2nd Division had fared very differently. Their line transected the road to Sevastopol with its bridge, which was swept by Russian guns. The advance was a case of moving from garden-wall to field-wall to take cover, although casualties were heavy (though not as heavy as those of the Light Division).[8] The Russians had set fire to the houses in the village of Burlyuk near the bridge, so the 2nd Division was split into two or rather three. The most western battalion became mixed up with Codrington's Brigade, the next three battalions including De Lacy Evans and staff (and no doubt Fox) went to the left of the burning houses, while the last two, who went to the right, crossed the river downstream. The main part of the 2nd Division was held up by the bridge until British artillery could be brought up to force the Russians to withdraw. By 5 p.m. the battle was over and the Russian army was in full retreat down the road to Sevastopol. Here is an account by a Russian participant which shows to what the enemy attributed their defeat:[9]

Each one of us felt his heart sink at the sight of the orderly advance of the endless mass of troops. However our artillery had taken up favourable positions and prepared to fire on the army but they started too early so the balls did not reach the enemy and only wasted ammunition. Our troops had set fire to the vineyards and village of Burlyuk near the sea. The smoke blew back on us, an evil portent. . . . The army came nearer and nearer so that our balls began to take effect but even when they came into artillery range and our cannon destroyed whole ranks yet still they came on as if not noticing and not caring about their dead comrades. Finally as they came almost into smallarms range so their deadly rifles (shtutsera) appeared on the scene, and from the sea thousands of balls hailed down, so that the Minsk Regiment, stationed by the sea for God knows what reason or purpose was annihilated in a few minutes. I speak of murderous rifles because every bullet told. . . .

Although only a fraction of the British Army was armed with rifles its superiority over the Russian arm was at once evident. It is probably fair to say that the British casualties were caused mainly by artillery, the Russian by smallarms. It can be given to few as it was to Fox, to see the weapon which he had so assiduously studied and taught, so triumphantly vindicated in the hands of his own pupils.

The staff of the 2nd Division suffered no fatalities but five were wounded including General De Lacy Evans himself. Fox was lucky to have escaped unscathed. The Lane Fox that Russell saw on a stretcher [10] was probably his cousin, who was wounded in the ankle. An incomplete account of the battle that he sent to his wife will be found in Appendix One.

No doubt the horrors of the battlefield have been much the same at all periods, but the lack of medical attention for the wounded made the Alma particularly unpleasant.[11] Russell slept in a tent on the battlefield on the night of the twentieth and the officers who shared it with him were frequently running out in response to cries from the wounded who littered the field. Russell was ill for several days afterwards. The 21st and 22nd of September were spent in burying the dead and taking the wounded to the coast to be taken off by ship.

The Alma was the only major action that Fox saw and it must have made a deep impression on him. In Lord Raglan's dispatch from Balaclava in which Division Commanders could nominate officers for special commendation, among the names of those of whom Evans 'eulogizes the conduct'[13] was Fox. A staff officer was of course under the eye of the Commander and perhaps therefore had a special advantage. In December his promotion to Brevet Major was for distinguished service in the field.[14]

On 23 September the army moved south when after some hesitation a decision had been taken to make a circuitous course round the east of Sevastopol so as to invest it from the south. The Allied armies took up their siege positions before Sevastopol in late September. This time the French were on the left and the English on the right, with the 2nd Division on the extreme right. The first fortnight of October was spent in unloading guns for the Allied bombardment that began on 17 October, but Fox had left the Crimea before this began[15] since a medical examination on 15 October had shown that he was unfit for service.

Although he spent a bare month in the Crimea—from 14 September to 15 October—Fox saw the best part of the war and missed the inconclusive battles of Balaclava and Inkermann, the appalling winter that followed and the humiliations of 1855. His Crimea medal had clasps for the Alma and Sevastopol, while he earned the Turkish medal and the Turkish Order of Medjidie, 5th Class. This month of active service was no doubt the most memorable of his military career.

He must have sailed directly back to England for on 9 November Johnny Stanley wrote to his mother: 'I suppose you heard Fox was home, I saw him yesterday. I hardly knew him, he is quite sallow and had a beard—he looks rather seedy.'[16] Alice and Augustus evidently stayed at Lady Caroline's house in Chesham Place.

In about May of 1855 Fox returned to Malta and was followed soon after by his wife who was expecting a child.[17] His return to Malta was caused by the revival of the intention to create a school of musketry in the Mediterranean, the object being to re-equip the whole army in the Crimea with the P.53 (Enfield) rifle of which large quantities were being sent to Malta.[18] The couple spent just over two years in Malta during which time two sons were born to Alice. It was intended to call the first child (born on 2 November 1855) Alexander St George to the indignation of Alice, her mother and grandmother: 'Alexander wished by Col. Gorden and Aug. St George is after the new ranges at Malta which were finished at the time of his birth but at which Fox has not yet practised . . .'.[19] The second child (St George) was born on 14 September 1856, which prompted Lady Maria Josepha to remark: 'Two babies in a nursery under a year old is really too much happiness for the most ardent baby fancier.'[20]

We have little evidence about his activities in Malta. He was evidently engaged mainly in training and Johnny Stanley recorded the high reputation he had among officers who had been there for the skill with which he managed the men. He was also testing the Enfield and Lancaster.[21] His promotion as Lieutenant-Colonel came in May 1857. On the other hand he was severely criticized in print by Hay at Hythe for his elaborate training methods limiting training to only a small proportion of the troops in Malta.

The family returned to England in early August 1857 and Lady

Stanley remarked: 'the children look lean and pale but I dare say they will soon pick up when they get to Alderley'.[22] Lord Stanley commented:

Fox seems of a discontented and querulous nature and expects some high post will immediately be offered to him and if not he is very ill used. I cannot see why he shld. not go back to his duty in the Regt., like many other officers who had higher Staff offices than he has had and who do not consider it a hardship to do Regimental duty.[23]

The criticism of his training methods in Malta had evidently made him ineligible for anything except regimental duties, but Lord Stanley did not understand the position.

The family had installed itself at Lord Stanley's house in Dover Street much to Stanley's chagrin. Matters were complicated by the fact that Alice was again expecting a child and on 10 December Stanley remarked: 'If Alice's house is much longer delayed she will pup in the street'.[24]

The child was born on 9 January 1858 in Brompton Crescent, apparently in lodgings,[25] but they found a house soon after for he (it was a son) was christened on 24 March at St James Church, Clapham Park.[26] Two further children were baptised in 1861 and 1862 at the same church (Ursula Katherine, born 27.8.1859, was baptised elsewhere). The family lived at Park Hill House (now demolished) between Park Hill and Clapham Park Road. Although south of the river this was a well-to-do area, albeit much less fashionable than where they had been accustomed to reside. They lived here until 1862 when Fox was posted to Ireland and they then probably made use of his mother's house at 1, Chesham Street.

On 5 December 1860 Kate Stanley wrote: 'We heard yesterday that Alice was very ill with a nervous fever, which they are afraid may turn to typhus; it has been brought on by excitement about the enquiry that is now going on about Augustus'.[27] The inquiry referred to was evidently the efforts made by Fox to vindicate himself after the criticisms made by Hay. These had been at first interpreted as insubordination but the efforts of his Regimental Commanding officer, Lt. Col. Lindsay, seemed to have caused the matter to be reconsidered.[27a] Sir John Pennefather the Commanding Officer in Malta said that he had been responsible for the methods of training in Malta and so took the blame away from Fox. He seems to have been cleared by the latter part of 1861.

It was in the later 1850s that Fox began to frequent the United Service Institution, later the Royal United Service Institution.[28] This had been founded in 1831 'as a central Repository for objects of Professional Art, Science and Natural History and for Books and Documents relating to those studies, or of general information. The delivery of Lectures on appropriate subjects is included in the design of the Institution.' Lectures were begun in 1849 and a journal to record them started in 1857. Favourite subjects were surveying, the rifle and antiquarian matters. In 1858 the Institution was divided into five departments: the Library and Reading Rooms; the Military Department; the Naval Department; Ethnological Department and Antiquities; the Natural History Department. There were a large number of models and in this year Colonel Hamilton of the Grenadier Guards (we have made frequent use of his history of the regiment published in 1874) had placed his model of the siege of Sevastopol and the south of the Crimea in the Institution. This then was another occasion (apart from Sandhurst) when Fox encountered a large number of models. More important still was the fact that the Institution possessed one of the largest ethnographic collections in the country, although it had been reduced in 1857. Fox lectured to the Institution on the rifle in 1858 and 1861 but by 1867 he was lecturing on ethnographic matters. The transference of his interests from one subject to the other was no doubt due partly to the facilities provided by the Institution itself.

On 14 June 1858 the introductory lecture of a general series entitled 'On the Improvement of the Rifle as a Weapon for General Use' was given at the Institution by Fox. His task was to give the history of the introduction of the rifle. It was one of his finest lectures and is indeed probably still the best introduction to that subject. He revealed that he had kept a private journal from 1851–57 during the testing at Woolwich, Enfield, Hythe and Malta. Numerous contrivances had been put forward for the improvement of the musket but only a few serve 'as links in the chain of progress, whilst others have branched out of the main line and contributed nothing of permanent utility.' His remarks were confined to the 'main chain of improvement, disregarding all those varieties which, however ingenious in themselves, have embodied no principle of practical benefit to our own times.' We need not follow the substance of the lecture but one memorable phrase is worth quoting:

the path of improvement has been stumbled upon and followed by those who were in search of something widely remote from it . . . showing that in all things necessity, rather than foresight, has been the mother of invention.

Some of these remarks had clearly been prompted by experience during the formation of his own collection.

On 20 May 1861 he spoke 'On a Model Illustrating the Parabolic Theory of Projection for ranges in Vacuo.' The trajectory of a bullet is influenced by three forces, the explosion, gravity and air resistance. The third was imponderable and so the model ignored it and illustrated the trajectory 'in vacuo.' He had worked out the model at Hythe, and it would evidently have been a very useful instructional aid.

The evidence of John Stanley, the *Instruction of Musketry* and the lecture just referred to all suggest that Fox had a considerable aptitude or even flare for teaching, adult teaching at all events. However, the instructor grade in the army was Captain, so he soon became too senior to do much teaching himself. In later life he was regarded very much as the scholar's scholar who would make no concession to ignorance and it is therefore interesting to contrast this with his youthful years.

In 1861 Mason and Slidell were arrested on board the British ship *Trent* by the Union authorities, the 'Trent case' of the American Civil War. The British Government responded by sending the 1st Battalion of Grenadier Guards and the 2nd Battalion of Scots Fusiliers to Canada. 'Previous to this departure of the Battalion Lieutenant-Colonel Augustus Lane Fox, of the Grenadier Guards, had on the 2nd of December, been sent out to Canada on "special service".' We have no information about how he fared in Canada although the 'special service' was presumably training in the use of the rifle.[29]

In August 1862 he was appointed Assistant Quartermaster General for the southern district of Ireland at Cork. Possibly he owed the appointment to Lord Stanley, or possibly the posting was not much sought after but Fox was attracted by the comparative freedom that it offered him. Ireland had then a considerable English garrison and Cork was the headquarters of their southern district. The large barracks were on a hill above Glanmore Road on the east side of the town and could hold 1,000 cavalry and four regiments of infantry.

We have no direct knowledge of Fox's manner of life in Ireland although he had his family there with him for two of his children were born there. He used his mother's house in Chesham Street as his London address and he presumably spent a good deal of his time in the capital. These four years in Ireland were extremely formative in Fox's professional career, or possibly it would be more accurate to say this is where he began it. He did his first fieldwork there and probably made the first draft of *Primitive Warfare*. The Irish ambience seems to have stimulated him in a way that strangely recalls the similar experience of Anthony Trollope in Government service in Ireland a few years earlier. It was as if the relaxed atmosphere of a Celtic country acted as a balm on English inhibitions.

Something will be said in the next chapter about the influence of Wilde's Catalogue on Fox's ideas about artefact study, and in the following chapter about the 6-inch Ordnance Survey maps available for the past 20 years in Ireland but not yet in southern England. He bore much greater authority than he had had previously and seems to have had a special responsibility for coastal defences which no doubt caused him to revise his surveying techniques.[29 a]

There was a more sombre side to his duties. After the end of the American Civil War returning Irish Americans stimulated the Fenian movement in Ireland. Surprisingly a number of solders with long service in the British Army took the oath of Irish Republican Brotherhood. In 1866 Fox was prosecuting officer of two NCO's, Drum Major Butler and Sergeant Darragh, charged with treason, Fenian conspiracy, at their Courts Martial.[29b] The offences, mainly drilling other Fenians, seem very mild in modern eyes. Fox had a more general responsibility of reporting to the authorities on the growth of Fenianism in southern Ireland, which prompted him to some general reflections on Irish troubles. Essentially he regarded the problem as social and ethnic, not political, as contemporaries thought—a view which we would no doubt endorse today.

In July 1867 Fox went on half-pay[30] and so was free of military duties for the next six years. He left with the rank of Colonel and went to live in a large semi-detached house at 10 Upper Philimore Gardens, behind Kensington High Street at the foot of Campden Hill. Both house and promotion[31] had been purchased with money provided by his mother (Lady Caroline lived until 1873).

Looking back over his 22 years of active military service what strikes us as important? He had travelled widely: the Continent (1852), Malta, Turkey, Bulgaria and the Crimea (1854), Malta (1855–7), Canada (1861–2) and Ireland (1862–66). About two-fifths of his service had been abroad (Ireland was strictly speaking a home-posting), and so had greatly widened his horizons. He was probably not greatly inclined towards normal regimental duties and his involvement with the rifle provided a release from this, as well as furnishing a subject to which he could dedicate himself. Fox was by temperament not a man to be satisfied with career and family; in Ireland he found new interests to which he could devote the rest of his life.

EVOLUTION

The first edition of *On the Origin of Species by Means of Natural Selection* appeared in November, 1859 and was followed by a second edition in January, 1860. The book was the subject of discussion all over the country and we can be reasonably certain that it was a matter of controversy among the young Stanleys.[1] Fox was in London at the time and no doubt read it soon after publication. The book or the consequences that flowed from it re-orientated his life, although its significance was not apparent to him for two or three years. To understand this we must return to Ireland.

When Fox arrived in Ireland the last of the three volumes of the Catalogue of the Museum of the Royal Irish Academy had just appeared: *Stone, Earthen and Vegetable Materials* (1857), *Animal Materials and Bronze* (1861), *Gold* (1862). The author of this remarkable catalogue, William Robert Wills Wilde, was a surgeon by profession although a distinguished antiquary as well. As a classification by date was not possible he adopted a primary classification by material and a secondary division by use: 'The classification and arrangement usually employed in Natural History according to Class, Order, Species and Variety, has, for the sake of convenience been adopted.' To illustrate the point: Class I—stone materials, with orders (1) flint, (2) stone, (3) crystal; Class II—Earthen materials, with orders (1) clay and pottery, (2) glass and enamel. The secondary division by use consisted of: (1) Weapons—offensive and defensive . . . (2) Tools and Weapon-Tools; flint flakes etc. . . . etc. up to 12 categories.

Whether Fox knew Wilde personally is uncertain but it is unlikely that he met him except possibly socially, not professionally. At all events the system curiously recalls that used by Fox himself. According to his view collections could be classified geographically (like Christy's) or by form, like his and like Wilde's. The insistence of Fox on classifying material culture as in biology (particularly in the 1860s) again recalls Wilde's catalogue. Fox had been impressed by the constant process of change in the weapons he knew, but if the whole of material culture could be classified on a kind of Linnean system then the change recognized by Fox might be operating in a way analogous to the natural selection that Darwin had shown had moulded and was moulding the living world. Looked at in this way what had been a matter of convenience for Wilde could become a key to the understanding of human material culture.

What for Fox had been a hobby—albeit a very serious one—now by analogy with Darwinian evolution took on quite a different status. The linear series of the development of artefacts might be arranged in a great family tree to reveal the course of the evolution of human material culture as a whole. For a man with the sense of dedication of Fox this was a challenge that had to be taken up. It was this change in status of his studies that was the most important influence of Darwinian evolution upon him. Much of his later life, including the Cranborne Chase episode, is unintelligible unless this is realized.

In the 1860s Fox tended to adopt Darwinian views in a crude form, and his ideas were profoundly modified to fit them. This is why it is always extremely rash to believe that he held the same views in the 1850s as he did in the 1860s or 1870s. From the 1870s Fox tended to change his allegiance to Herbert Spencer from whom he had received a favourable mention of his collection in 1874 in *The Principles of Sociology*, I.[2] Both men were inclined to regard themselves as hard done by, unrecognised savants who had discerned the reality of evolution before the *Origin*. Nevertheless Fox's activities and achievements would have been unthinkable outside the climate of opinion produced by the publication of the *Origin of Species*.

Evolution was controversial in 1860s but generally accepted by 1870. It was during the controversial period that Fox found himself associated with two men, both close friends of Darwin, who were at the heart of the movement (if we may use such a term). They were Sir John Lubbock and Thomas Huxley, the former to be associated with Fox for the rest of his life, the latter for only a short period. None of the three men had had a higher education and were self-taught in the Victorian sense of the word.

While he was stationed in Ireland in October 1863 Fox was put forward for Fellowship of the Society of Antiquaries of London.[3] His qualification was 'an attachment to the study of antiquities especially ancient arms and armour.' Among his sponsors were Albert Way, Augustus Franks (of the British Museum) and Henry Christy. He was duly elected in June of the following year as was Sir John Lubbock. If they did not know each other already they probably met soon afterwards.

Born in 1834, Lubbock had disliked the Classical education given at Eton and left at the age of 14 to go into his father's bank in the City.[4] Since boyhood Darwin had lived near his home and he studied under him; indeed, according to his biographer, Darwin had moulded Lubbock's character.[5] He achieved a precocious scientific reputation and was elected a Fellow of the Royal Society in his mid-twenties. He had been interested in archaeology and was involved in the events that led up to the acceptance of the antiquity of man. A series of articles that he had published in the *Natural History Review* (of which he was Editor and possibly owned) were drawn together in *Prehistoric Times* (first edition, 1865) which ran through many editions in the latter part of the century. He entered Parliament in 1870 and introduced a number of reforms: August Bank Holiday, Early Closing, the Ancient Monuments Protection, and so on, by private bill (of the last we must say more later). He loved social life and at his week-end parties at High Elms, Kent, Gladstone and other notable political and social figures were entertained. He was of a much more sociable disposition than Fox, skilled in persuading people to do what he wanted them to do, although he lacked the application and sense of dedication of Fox. After he had become a widower Lubbock met Alice Fox-Pitt (Fox's second daughter) at Castle Howard in 1882 and they were married in 1884, and thus Lubbock became the son-in-law of Fox.

Lubbock and Huxley were of course well known to each other; both belonged to the X Club which had a powerful influence on the affairs of the Royal Society. Both had spoken at the famous meeting of the British Association at Oxford in 1860 in support of evolution. Huxley who is too well known to need describing here was far the most brilliant of the Darwinians and with that penchant for controversy that is common among academics had set himself up as the champion of Darwin. At this time he enjoyed a much closer contact with Darwin than Lubbock, to whom he acted as general adviser. Huxley was of course a zoologist. Soon after the publication of the *Origin* which had not taken man into account Huxley published *Man's Place in Nature* (1863). It was a morphological comparison of the four anthropoid apes with man, which he had been urged it could be unwise to publish. He concluded: 'And after passion and prejudice have died away, the same result will attend the teachings of the naturalist respecting that great Alps and Andes of the living world—Man. Our reverence for the nobility of manhood will not be lessened by the knowledge that man is, in substance and in structure, one with the brutes . . .'.[6] Although he was associated with him for a shorter period it is likely that the intellectual power of Huxley made a much greater impact upon Fox than the longer association with Lubbock.

The forum within which the three men met was the Ethnological Society of London. This ephemeral body existed only for the decade 1860–70; it had been formed by a secession from the Anthropological Society with which it re-united in 1870. By reason of their travels military men had often acquired an interest in ethnology and when Fox joined the Society in 1861 he found many soldiers among the membership. Lubbock joined later and shortly after became Secretary and then President.

It may be wondered how Huxley became involved with the

Ethnological Society. His primary interest was in physical anthropology. Biology was divided into the two great departments of botany and zoology, anthropology being one of the divisions of zoology, and ethnology one of its sub-divisions.[7]

Ethnology is the science which determines the distinctive characters of the persistent modifications of mankind; which ascertains the distribution of these modifications in present and past times and seeks to discover the causes, or conditions of existence, both of the modifications and their distribution.

After Fox went on half-pay in 1867 he was able to devote his full energies to his professional interests. In 1868 the 3rd Session of the International Congress of Prehistoric Archaeology was held at Norwich and London. Fox was Secretary of the Committee of Organization, General Secretary and Chairman of the Publication Committee.[8] Although he did not make any very impressive contribution to the papers it is fair to say that he organized the whole business. It gave him an opportunity to meet many leading biologists and geologists (Huxley, Hooker, Lyell—Lubbock was President—and others).

Following this there was something of an upheaval in the Ethnological Society with an elaborate new constitution of which there can be little doubt Fox was the author. Below the President (Huxley) was a General Secretary (Fox), a Foreign Secretary with a Deputy Secretary for India, and Secretaries for Philology, Archaeology, Biology and Comparative Psychology. In addition there were local secretaries, a Treasurer and two paid officers. There is a decidedly military flavour about this elaborate constitution.

This organisation had only a short life since at the formation of the Institute in 1870 neither Huxley nor Fox were retained in office. Nevertheless during this short period the Society, which became a vehicle for Fox's ideas, was involved in preservation of monuments and in prehistoric archaeology. At this period he adopted the most extreme Darwinian position. The quotation below is from a long comment he made on a paper on megaliths given at the Society on 9 February 1869 with Huxley in the chair:

The more we examine into the culture of the primitive inhabitants of the globe, the more we perceive it to have expanded and developed upon a plan analogous to that which has been observed in the development of species, and the more evident it becomes that the method of investigating these memorials should be the same systematic method which we employ for investigating the phenomena of the animal and vegetable kingdoms.[9]

When Fox was posted to Ireland in 1862 his collection was 10 years old. Nothing is known of its extent at that date because he had still not published anything on it. The fact that Christy (p. 32) was one of his sponsors at the Antiquaries suggests that Fox had been under his influence for some time and that his interests had already turned towards antiquity. That this was so is indicated by his first essays in fieldwork in Ireland. So far as we know he had shown no interest in fieldwork or field monuments before this date.

We know that he went on half-pay at the age of 40 in 1867 at his own request,[9a] and it is not unreasonable to suppose that one purpose of this was to devote himself to the scientific study of antiquity. His decision to go on a prolonged period of fieldwork in the Wolds (where he met Canon Greenwell) just before this lends weight to this suggestion.[9b] That will be discussed in the next chapter, for here we are concerned with his studies arising largely from his own collection. Of these the first three, the three lectures on Primitive Warfare delivered in June, 1867, 1868, 1869 at the Royal United Service Institution, were almost certainly conceived while he was in Ireland.

After 1869 there was a pause of five years before Fox gave a series of further important lectures. His collection had been put on display at the Bethnal Green Museum and he published a catalogue of part of the collection (Catalogue Pt. I and II was published in 1874 and re-issued in 1877; Pts. III and IV, although prepared for publication, never appeared). When the Anthropological Institute visited the collection in 1874 he lectured on 'The Principles of Classification' and in the same year he also lectured on 'Early Modes of Navigation.' In 1875 he lectured at the Royal Institution on 'The Evolution of Culture' (see Appendix Two), the climax of the series and also his last major talk of this kind. From 1875 onwards, as we shall see, his main interest had shifted to fieldwork. The rest of this chapter will be devoted to a discussion of these six lectures and the catalogue.[10]

The lectures are interesting in being the nearest that Fox came to a theoretical work. He was essentially a practical man, a pragmatist, who never wrote a general work in his life. He was not averse to theory, as we can see in his work on the rifle, but his training had been in something where results—the score on the target—were what mattered. What he had noticed—a continuity in development of various objects by gradual modification—had in the light of Darwinian evolution become no longer a hobby but the key to the study of the whole of human material culture. When reading the lectures, then, we occasionally feel that we hear the voice of a prophet.

The first three of them are twice as long as the second three and if delivered as published must have lasted for nearly two hours each. Clearly the result of prolonged study, they differ in other respects from the later three. They were of course in sequence. There is markedly more Darwinian influence and the *Origin* is frequently quoted or referred to in the earlier series but in the later lectures the debt to Herbert Spencer is more.

The three lectures on 'Primitive Warfare' follow the development of warfare from its pre-human origin in the animal kingdom, through the Stone Age in the second lecture to the early age of metal in the last one. Adopting the terminology of phrenology (in which Fox was interested, p. 19) three basic instincts are implanted in higher animals, '... alimentiveness, for the sustenance of life; amativeness, for the propagation of species; and combativeness, for the protection of species, and the propagation by natural selection of the most energetic breeds; on which latter subject much important information has been given to the world by Mr Darwin, in his celebrated work on the origin of species.'[11] The origin of warfare is therefore to be found in natural selection and the struggle for survival. If this was the cause of warfare it is not surprising that the development of the instruments used in it were governed by similar principles.

Among animals and savages weapons fall into three categories: defensive (hides, solid plates etc.), offensive (piercing, striking etc.) strategem, (flight, concealment etc.).[12] In the case of animals of course the weapon of defence or offence, the shell or horn, is an organic growth on the beast, but in the case of man it was an imitation of what he had seen in the animal world and improved. The lecture is therefore largely concerned with primitive weapons of offence or defence (he did not deal with stratagems) that appear to imitate the organic weapons of the lower animals.

The second lecture has a very valuable preface:

We come into the world helpless and speechless, possessing only in common with the brutes such instincts as are necessary for the bare sustenance of life under the most facile conditions; all that follows afterwards is dependent purely on experience.[13]

How then did we manage to rise above such a state? First, of course, by imitation of nature as described in the first lecture, but second by accidental variation among tools or objects being made:

Occasionally some form would be hit upon, which in the hands of its employer would be found more convenient for use, and which, by giving the possessor of it some advantage over his neighbours, would commend itself to general adoption. Thus by a process, resembling what Mr Darwin, in his late work, has termed 'unconscious selection', rather than by pre-meditation or design, men would be led on to improvement.[14]

Gradually some tools would be better adapted for certain purposes than others. In the long run however there would be continuity of development. To recover the evidence to demonstrate this continuity is the daunting task that the lecturer had set himself:

The difficulty that we have to contend with is precisely that which the geologist experiences in tracing his palaeontological sequence. But it is far greater, for natural history has long been studied, and the materials upon which Mr.

Darwin formed his celebrated hypothesis have been in process of collection for many generations. But continuity, in relation to the arts, can scarcely yet be said to be established as a science.[15]

The rest of the lecture is then devoted to prehistoric stone implements and modern primitive weapons in organic materials (shields, clubs, boomerangs). In modern eyes the figures of sequences of flint tools are a little jejune, since resemblances between tools of flint can be so often purely accidental. In the case of the ethnological objects he was breaking new ground, particularly boomerangs (in which Fox was especially interested and in which he had carried out experiments) and Australian shields.

In his third lecture Fox was confronted with a different problem. He was dealing with the first metal weapons or tools, of bronze in some areas like Europe and the Middle East but of iron in central and southern Africa, for he recognised that a bronze age was not universal. Copper might have been introduced independently in different areas but bronze, an alloy of copper with tin (a rare metal, not commonly found in the same area as copper) could hardly have been stumbled upon accidentally in several places. This led him to a discussion of independent invention and diffusion, in which he was too shrewd an observer to tie himself to the former. This discussion which is still very relevant today contains many memorable passages of which we can only quote a few:

A batter pudding is composed of milk, flour and eggs, in proper proportions, but a careless cook will constantly vary her proportions, and will fail in adjusting her quantities to the total amount; but we must not, on that account, assume that each cook has invented the art of making batter puddings independently.[16]

. . . there is no more fruitful source of error than the attempt to apply ancient history and tradition to the elucidation of prehistoric events. Modern science, and our fuller appreciation of the value of evidence, have thrown far more light on prehistoric times than ever fell to the lot of the ancients; and it is for us, therefore, to correct their errors, and not to be misled by them.[17]

Whatever degree of veracity we may be disposed to attribute to early history, we must at least admit that the implements have this advantage over written testimony of any kind, that they cannot intentionally mislead us. If we draw wrong inferences from them, the fault is our own.[18]

After nearly six years on half pay Fox returned to full-time soldiering in early 1873, taking command of the West Surrey Brigade Depot at Guildford, so that his very large anthropological collection became an embarrassment. In June 1874 it was placed on exhibition in the Bethnal Green branch of the South Kensington Museum, and it was transferred to the main museum in 1878.

From 1874 to 1884 it was a private collection on public exhibition, but we know from the surviving receipts from the Museum[18a] that it was not a static collection. Indeed Pitt-Rivers was pouring material into it, a great deal of it fresh purchases. After 1880 his newly-acquired inheritance gave much greater freedom of purchasing. In order to settle its future Pitt-Rivers offered it to the nation. The Government set up a committee to consider the offer, composed it may be mentioned largely of Fox's friends (Lubbock, Huxley, Rolleston, etc.), who recommended acceptance. It was turned down however on the grounds that it was an ethnological collection and that the British Museum, not South Kensington, dealt with ethnology. Pitt-Rivers of course contended that it was much more than this, a demonstration of the development of the arts, but as he had called it an ethnological collection in his original offer the Government case could hardly be contested.

After the refusal of the authorities to retain the collection at South Kensington it was offered to Oxford University, which accepted it. A few years later it was put on display in a newly-built annexe to the University Museum where it is still housed, albeit now altered out of all recognition. The rebuff by the Government to Pitt-Rivers over his offer naturally rankled for many years.

The 1874 Catalogue explained that the objects were similar to those found in other museums but 'only in relation to their psychological and sociological bearings' was there an improvement. In his writings of this later period Fox drew heavily upon Spencer, as he himself admitted. It had been thought that objects of this type could only be arranged geographically and Christy, whose large collection had influenced Fox considerably, had arranged his collection in that way. Since 1852 Fox had been collecting the common types of object and arranging them in sequence to illustrate 'the successive ideas by which the minds of men in a primitive condition of culture have progressed in the development of their arts from the simple to the complex, and from the homogeneous to the heterogeneous.' The function of the anthropologist is to trace back the sequence to its source:

Human ideas, as represented by the various products of human industry, are capable of classification into genera, species, and varieties in the same manner as the products of the vegetable and animal kingdoms, and in their development from the homogeneous to the heterogeneous they obey the same laws.

The collection itself was divided into four parts: I, skulls and hair; II, Weapons; III Miscellaneous arts of modern savages including Early Modes of Navigation; IV, Prehistoric series. The greater part of the catalogue deals with weapons: Shields, Body armour, Head-dresses, Knives, Daggers and Swords. Each of the 21 sections has a description and an introduction. It is still a very valuable book for the student of material culture who is lucky enough to possess a copy.

His lecture in December to the Anthropological Institute on 'Early Modes of Navigation' gives us some clue as to a section of Part III of his

Catalogue. He divided the subject into seven categories: (1) solid trunks or dug-outs developing into, (2) vessels on which planks are laced, later plugged and nailed; (3) bark canoes; (4) vessels of skin and wicker work; (5) rafts, developing into, (6) outrigger canoes and later vessels of broader beam; (7) rudders, sails and contrivances which gave rise to more advanced parts of vessels. As a general account of primitive navigation it has not been bettered although on some points, such as the origin of the outrigger, modern opinion might not fully endorse the views expressed.

At the opening of the exhibition Fox gave an introductory talk on the 'Principles of Classification' that he had employed to the members of the Anthropological Institute. The normal geographic arrangement was more strictly ethnological since it illustrated the arts of various peoples; his arrangement by form illustrated the development of specific ideas and was of greater sociological value. In an individual repeated actions went through two stages: first when the intellect had to be concentrated in order to carry it out, and then when by repetition it became automatic. The original ideas have vanished but the objects themselves remain; in studying them this movement from new effort to old effortless repetition has to be borne in mind. Selection from the multitude in the first category for what passed into the second was controlled by utility operating as a sort of natural selection among the struggling ideas:

... what I conceived to be the object of an anthropological collection is to trace out, by means of the only evidence available, the sequence of ideas by which mankind has advanced from the condition of the lower animals to that in which we find him at the present, and by this means to provide really reliable materials for a philosophy of progress. ... Affording us as they do the only available evidence of man in his most primitive condition, they are well worthy of our attention, in order that by studying their grammar, we may be able to conjugate their forms[21].

Of course only durable remains have survived from the prehistoric period, so for tools of perishable materials we must turn to modern primitive peoples. Their material culture did not seem to be a degeneration of higher cultures but quite an independent development. Australian material culture appeared to copy nature rather than higher cultures of other areas. In this lecture he discussed bows and particularly the composite bow of Eurasia. It is paradoxical that it is precisely when Fox abandoned forms and studied geographical distribution (with bows, the boomerang, primitive boats) that he made some of his most valuable contributions to the study of material culture.

Language has been studied scientifically for some time. The data is much easier to handle, written as it is on paper unlike the space occupied by hundreds of specimens of an anthropological collection. Yet in the early periods it is untrustworthy, 'Whilst in the earliest phases of humanity the names for things change with every generation if not more frequently, the things themselves are handed down unchanged from father to son and from tribe to tribe . . .'.

In the study of material culture

> Progress is like a game of dominoes—like fits on to like. In neither case can we tell beforehand what will be the ultimate figure produced by the adhesions; all we know, is that the fundamental rule of the game is sequence.

On 28 May 1875 Fox was invited to lecture at the Royal Institution, a considerable honour, and the title he chose was 'The Evolution of Culture.' It was the climax and end of the series with a title that well epitomized their basis. Some of it covered the same ground as the previous one and like that is written in a philosophical vein with a good deal of borrowing from Spencer. Fox had first to demonstrate that the study of material culture was a science in its own right, as much as the study of language or the physical sciences:

> . . . The principles of variation and natural selection have established a band of union between the physical and culture sciences which can never be broken. History is but another term for evolution. . . . But our position with regard to culture has always been one which has forced on our comprehension the reality of progress, whilst with respect to the slow progress of external nature it has been concealed from us, owing to the brief span of human existence and our imperfect records of the past.[22]

He then goes on to make a very skilful comparison between language and material culture to which we cannot do justice here, 'Modifications of words, like modifications in the forms of the arts, result from the succession of ideas or their causes affecting particular minds. They obtain acceptance through natural selection by the survival of the fittest.'[23] Under the primitive conditions tools have greater stability than words. He then goes over fairly familiar ground: the origin of flint and metal tools. (**24a, b,** pp. 148–9) shows the hypothetical derivation of Australian tools from a simple stick. He next cites cases of degeneration: coins derived from the stater of Philip of Macedon and decoration on paddle blades from New Ireland.

Apart from the Royal United Service Institution and Society of Antiquaries (of which he had been a member of Council and vice-President) Fox was also a Fellow of the Geological Society (to which he gave one lecture) and the Archaeological Institute. The main vehicles for his ideas were of course the Ethnological Society (later the Anthropological Institute) and the British Association for the Advancement of Science. This body had (and still has) a meeting of a week's duration each summer in one of the larger provincial cities where several hundred scientists gathered to hear lectures. It was something of a social occasion when friends renewed acquaintance, gossip was exchanged and business carried out. Most of his professional friends attended and from the late 1860s Fox rarely missed a meeting. He was

President of Section H, the Anthropology section in 1872 (Brighton) and 1888 (Bath). In 1876 Fox was elected a Fellow of the Royal Society, a fitting crown to the end of one part of his professional career.

According to the citation on his certificate of candidature[24] at the Royal Society Fox was 'Distinguished for his original researches into the development of Implements and Weapons and the origins of arts throughout the world, and eminent as a general Ethnologist and Archaeologist.' Seventeen Fellows sponsored him from personal knowledge, including Busk, Galton, Lubbock, Franks, Tylor, Prestwich and Evans. More interesting are the two Fellows who sponsored him from general knowledge: C. Darwin and A. L. Adams. He had received his accolade from the Master.

Darwin lived a very retired life at Down, visited by close friends like Huxley or Hooker but rarely himself attending meetings. He carried on a voluminous correspondence and he no doubt exchanged letters with Fox over the Notes for Travellers in Foreign Lands of the British Association, of which Fox was Editor and Darwin a contributor. There is no evidence that the two men ever met. In this instance Lubbock, who lived near Down, possibly had canvassed him.

Separated from his collection and with his main interest now in fieldwork, Fox rarely returned to this subject in the last 25 years of his life. The only recorded occasion was in a lecture to the Society of Arts in December, 1891, where the earlier collection at Oxford was compared with his new collection at Farnham.

'I hold that the great desideratum of our day is an educational museum in which the visitors may instruct themselves. . . . The law that nature makes no jumps. . . . The knowledge of the facts of evolution, and of the processes of gradual development is the one great knowledge that we have to inculcate . . .'. Recourse must be had to sequence of type 'and that is what I term "typology. . .". Typology forms a tree of progress and distinguishes the leading shoots from the inner branches. The problems of the naturalist and thus of the typologist are analogous.'

We have all noticed that this year's model of a motor-car differs from last year's and similarly next year's model will be different from that. If one arranges models from each year back to the first motor-car, ultimately a vehicle is reached that looks like a horse-drawn carriage. Then the same thing could be done and the sequence of models of horse-drawn carriages could be arranged to show their origin, and so on. This of course can be done with spoons, boots, furniture, houses or anything you like. What Fox maintained was that every object of human manufacture could be fitted into a sequence of this kind and if you followed the sequences backwards ultimately they converged, the forms becoming simpler and simpler until you reached the first human artefacts. Indeed you could go beyond this and in 'Primitive Warfare' we are shown how the ultimate prototypes were to be found in the animal kingdom.

The modern museum curator may owe the word 'typology' to Fox, but he uses it in a much more restricted sense than Fox would have done. He regarded typology as the key to the whole of human material culture, not as we use it for arranging a limited number of objects in a sequence to illustrate their development. For Fox it was a philosophy, not simply a convenient display method.

The matter is extremely important in understanding Fox's motivation in other spheres such as fieldwork or preservation. He had a self-assurance derived from a vision of the unity of the past. When he went out to excavate it was with a view to finding objects to fit into his sequence, or to create a new one. His purpose was to find objects not to display in a cabinet but to relate to a general scheme and thereby fit the monument itself into a chronological framework. In the next chapter it will be shown that the purpose of his excavation later changed at the same time as his interest in the 'evolution of culture' slackened.

It will be appreciated that a scheme of this kind had its main value as an instrument for studying the past before written records—the prehistoric period. Hitherto although remains of these periods had been known they were, if not inaccessible to study, at least very reluctant to yield any worthwhile information. Fox's method of study gave them a fresh significance and made a new unity between history and the unwritten past. He himself was especially interested in the prehistoric past and there is no doubt that his particular concern with the preservation of prehistoric monuments owed something to his vision of that period.

As the nineteenth century advanced evolutionary ideas swept into most fields of thought, and probably they would have entered into the study of material culture even without Fox. Nevertheless the typological study of objects that today comes as second nature to the archaeologist or anthropologist must be in part attributed to Fox's evolutionary ideas. Sometimes—as with the late Abbé Breuil's examples of the degeneration of palæolithic art—there is a direct inspiration from the degeneration of the human form on the paddles from New Ireland demonstrated by Fox.

The question that must come to mind is: why if most people are prepared to follow Fox's methods are none, or very few, prepared to accept his general philosophy on the evolution of the culture? None of us has had the heady experience of encountering evolution for the first time as was the case in the mid-nineteenth century, or of coming under the direct influence of the disciples of Darwin, as did Fox. He was of course aware that artefacts cannot reproduce themselves, so that organic evolution must be very different from cultural evolution: it was the analogy that was overpowering, even if the mechanism was different. The subject is worthy of a great deal of discussion but we must confine ourselves to two points.

Changes in the organic world are imperceptible, but in human artefacts—at least in modern times—they are at once apparent. In the *Origin of Species* Darwin was making a case and his greatest stumbling block was precisely that people could not see evolution happening. He had to argue that it took place imperceptibly, so gradually that like the movement of the hands of the clock you could not perceive it. *Natura non saltum facit*: Nature makes no jumps or sudden moves—all change is gradual. Fox took over this outlook direct from Darwin, so far as we know modifying his own views to fit into it. Unlike Darwin, Fox did not have to prove change since everyone admitted it took place, and very obviously so in the mid-nineteenth century.

A criticism of the *Origin* made several times by Huxley was of this insistence on gradualness—'Mr. Darwin's position might, we think, have been even stronger than it is if he had not embarassed himself with the aphorism "Natura non facit saltum" which turns up so often in his pages. We believe, as we have said above that Nature does make jumps now and then . . .'.[26] If Darwin had taken this on unnecessarily, for Fox there was no justification at all for doing so. To take his starting point, the musket, its development in the seventeenth and eighteenth centuries was certainly slow, but at the time Fox became associated with it the invention of the expanding bullet by Delvigne had transformed its nature. Thus the development of the musket illustrates the weakness of the analogy made with organic evolution, for the invention of the expanding bullet was precisely one of those jumps that Fox argued did not occur.

Furthermore, improvements since then have altered the weapon almost beyond belief. Biologists may argue that evolution has proceeded at a uniform rate or in stops and starts, but none would maintain that there has been a continuous acceleration, as appears to be the case in the rate of development in material culture. No doubt among primitive peoples or with early man improvement is haphazard, a matter largely (but never entirely) of chance, but as the degree of conscious and rational endeavour increases with the passage of time so the rate of improvement accelerates. In organic evolution consciousness and reason of course play no part.

The second point is concerned with reproduction. Other naturalists before Darwin, notably Larmarck, had believed in evolution in the organic world, but none had been able to produce a convincing explanation of how it worked. The success of Darwin and Wallace was that they offered an explanation of great simplicity that rang true: natural seiection in a struggle for survival. But inanimate tools cannot reproduce themselves and do not engage in a struggle for survival. Fox struggled with this apparently insurmountable problem and indeed it still confronts the modern evolutionary anthropologist.

The most ingenious solution worked out by Fox was to replace natural selection by utility and to stage the conflict not between the tools but between the ideas in the mind of the toolmakers. We should remember that Fox had read Plato (p. 19). Among the myriads of ideas floating in the mind of the craftsman the iron law of utility weeded out the hosts of the weak and impractical. Although unconvincing (how can ideas struggle?) it is not a naive concept.

Fox's ideas sprang from seeds planted when he began his collection in the year following the Great Exhibition and which sprouted when they were fertilized and watered by the publication of the *Origin of Species*. They are profoundly Victorian in sentiment, but that is to be regarded as a compliment, not a criticism. Like one of Smiles's engineers Fox was a self-taught man; the strength and weakness of this is evident in his lectures. There is much shrewd observation and thought in them but like those engineers he was at his strongest not in the realm of theory but in the field of practice where we shall see him in the next four chapters.

V

EARLY FIELDWORK

Stationed in Malta as he was for over two years it is surprising that Fox never makes any mention of the famous temples of that island in his later work. There is indeed no clear evidence that he showed any interest in field monuments before he was posted to Ireland in August, 1862, as Assistant Quartermaster General at Cork. There is no hint of such an interest in the Stanley letters of the 1850s, nor does he ever refer in later lectures to antiquities he had seen on his foreign travels.

Our information about his four years in Ireland is scanty, although the papers recently presented to the Salisbury and South Wiltshire Museum show that as early as 1864 he was engaged in fieldwork in the area around Cork.[1] They also show that he had a special responsibility for coastal defences which no doubt made surveying necessary. Yet as I have pointed out (p. 29), it was clearly the point in his life when his views were completely re-orientated, under several influences besides the *Origin of Species*. He probably drafted the lectures on 'Primitive Warfare' while he was there; he did his first fieldwork there and seems for the first time to have become interested in preservation. Although in this book there are separate chapters on evolution, early fieldwork and preservation of ancient monuments, in fact his interest in all three seems to have started at that time.

So far as can be judged Fox worked in isolation in Ireland. He did not get on well with Irish antiquaries:

So much want of judgement has been shown in the treatment of Irish antiquities, and explorers had so often shown themselves to have been influenced by a spirit of political faction rather than a desire for truth, that the subject of Irish antiquities had fallen into disrepute. . . .[1a]

Ireland was the first part of the British Isles to be surveyed for maps at 6 in. to a mile (1824–42). Fox as AQMG at Cork had, of course, access to these new large-scale sheets, 'Thanks to the care taken by the officers of the Ordnance Survey of Ireland, under the direction of Lieutenant (now Colonel) Larcom, every rath* which then existed had been marked on the Government maps'; on these Fox had counted 10,000

---

* A circular enclosure made by an earthen bank, used as a fort or chief's residence.

raths in Munster.[2] He had gone out into the field and found more than half had gone (I assume Fox means more than half his sample). It was this fact that impressed upon his mind the degree of destruction taking place, while the ceaseless flow of gold objects to the Royal Irish Academy caused him to trust 'it might be made the subject of State interference before it was too late.'

This interest may have been the cause or the result of his work at Roovesmore Fort in 1865.[3] This was a rath, 130ft in diameter with a ditch 17ft wide and a bank on the outside. It contained an elbow-shaped souterrain inside. The capstones which were re-used uprights bore Ogham inscriptions of which two were legible. The venture seems to have been in the nature of a rescue operation since the local farmer was intending to destroy the site. The inscribed stones were taken to Cork and transported by sea to London to be housed at the British Museum. The local people—perhaps understandably—were very reluctant to assist in the removal of the stones.

The first glimpse we have of Fox's surveying is in the very small figures that illustrate his article. The resemblance is too close to later work to leave any doubt about the surveyor. He made use of a level for the sectional drawing with perpendiculars dropped at irregular intervals on significant points. It is the surveying used in military fortifications rather than architectural surveying but for this reason was probably better adapted to irregular earthworks.

In the latter part of 1866 Fox was back in London. He had read a short paragraph in the *Times* of 20 October reporting that 20 cartloads of bones had been removed from the site of an excavation for the foundations of a new wool warehouse to be built close to London Wall.[4] He went to investigate and visited daily during the next two months. A very large area had been opened up (224ft by 70ft). Undisturbed alluvial gravel lay at about 16ft and above it up to 6ft of peat covered by a layer of a filling of medieval and modern rubble up to ground surface. The bones (red deer, horse, wild boar, ox, roebuck, dog) came from the peat together with Roman leatherwork and metal-work and coins of Nerva, Vespasian, Trajan, Hadrian and Antoninus Pius. In the peat were upright piles. According to Fox there was a sequence of several stages: piles in the lower peat, midden in the peat, growth of peat, more piles, more midden and more peat. The piles, which varied in size from 6×8 in. to 4×3 in., presumably supported platforms for wharves of some kind over marshy floodable ground. The coins leave no doubt that the deposits belong to the early period of Roman London before the defences had been created. According to Fox similar piles had been found at New Southwark and elsewhere along the riverside.

This was one of the few waterlogged sites that Fox dug and it is clear that the enormous quantity of bone that was found permanently impressed upon his mind the importance of identification of animal bones, which became such a feature of his later work. He made a remark worthy of a modern adherent of *Rescue* and also indicative of his own feelings about preservation:

Thus while the remotest parts of Europe are being searched for the vestiges of lake dwellings and the most valuable reports on the same subject are received from the four quarters of the globe, similar remains are in daily process of destruction at our own doors by persons who are ignorant of their meaning, and of the importance that attaches to them.[5]

Fox went formally on half pay, apparently at his own request, on 6 July 1867, from when his time was his own. As part of his new dedication to the study of antiquity he had evidently decided the best course would be to excavate with someone who understood the business. Canon William Greenwell had published two articles on his barrow excavations in Yorkshire in the *Archaeological Journal* in 1865[6] and Fox had read of his work in the *Times* since he had a clipping from the paper.[6a] In April, 1867 he carried out extensive fieldwork in the Wolds (for which 6-in. maps existed) and also visited Greenwell's excavations while he was doing this.[7]

There could hardly have been a greater contrast between two men: on the one hand the aristocratic Colonel, veteran of the Alma, father of nine children and an evolutionist (when it was still controversial), and on the other a man of the cloth (or of the close one might say) and a bachelor. Greenwell (1820–1918) was seven years the senior of the two.[8] After taking his B.A. at Durham he travelled on the Continent and then became Curate at Burton Agnes in the East Riding. From 1854–1908 he was a Minor Canon at Durham where he made the fine collection of pre-Conquest stones. His main hobby was fishing but he also dug barrows. *British Barrows*, published in 1877, was written in collaboration with George Rolleston, who as we shall see became one of the closest of Fox's friends.

For Greenwell in 1865 the object of excavation was to throw light on the period from which there are no written records[9]:

It is impossible to reprobate too strongly that ignorant and greedy spirit of mere curiosity-hunting which has done—and alas! is still doing such injury to proper investigation of our ancient places of sepulture. The urn, the dagger and the arrowhead possess a very trifling interest and give us comparatively little information, unless we know the circumstances of their deposit.[10]

Fox was, then, the student of a man who took a very serious view of the purpose of excavation.

On his return to the south in the late summer Fox made a survey of the hillforts in Sussex.[11] He had no maps at a larger scale than 1 in. to a mile to help him (they were not yet available) and he made rough plans of the various hillforts (Seaford, Mt Caburn, Hollingbury, Whitchurch,

4 Cissbury Hill-fort, Sussex, looking east

Wolstenbury, Chanctonbury Ring and Cissbury) that he visited, travelling over this area 50 miles long and 5 miles wide on foot. He concluded the earthworks were isolated tribal defences. Cissbury, the largest camp in Sussex, was the object of special study. The works occupied the whole summit; water and fuel supplies were ignored; the size of the ramparts was inversely proportional to the natural strength of the place; ditch usually outside but sometimes inside; there were outworks, barbicans and an internal entrance; the inhabitants lived in pits; interior strewn with flints. This was the site chosen for excavation in September, 1867 and January, 1868.

It was the first formal excavation that Fox undertook. It is clear that he was very much at sea. 30 pits were dug not so much with the object of exploring the site but to provide flints to build up some of his series. The flints were found down to considerable depth and John Evans suggested the pits were flint mines. Fox was entirely pre-occupied with his series and was hardly able to think about structures:

Not withstanding the great difficulty of collecting the necessary materials for displaying a connected series of such forms ... this fundamental maxim is nevertheless capable of clear demonstration in any well-assorted collection of early and savage implements, and embodies, I believe, the pith and marrow of pretty nearly all that can be extracted from the study of prehistoric and comparative archaeology.

So long as he held views of this kind his excavation techniques were not likely to make a serious advance.

During the winter Greenwell came south, and evidently assisted Fox at Cissbury, doing some excavations there by himself. Fox had initiated a certificate for Greenwell for Fellowship of the Society of Antiquaries, but the original certificate shows that Fox's name has been struck out. Both men were of an irascible disposition and possibly Fox crossed out his name in anger after a quarrel (? over Cissbury). This might explain the mystery that seems to surround the relationship between the two men during this period. On the other hand they enjoyed an amicable relationship in later years, so possibly there is a quite innocent explanation for the erasure.

In 1868, as Secretary of the Organising Committee of the International Congress of Prehistoric Archaeology Fox must have been busy before its session in August, and afterwards in editing the papers. He found time however to do two pieces of fieldwork, that is riding or walking over the countryside, looking at antiquities and picking up flints or sherds.[12] He had been in the Oxford area in the Spring and in north Kent in September, where he had looked at monuments and also been led to believe that the association of flints with Roman pottery confirmed that the former were still in use in that period.

The extent of Fox's fieldwork in Ireland, Yorkshire, Sussex and elsewhere is sometimes overlooked. His sister-in-law, Kate Stanley, gives us a glimpse of him at work in 1869:

28 Aug. Augustus Fox comes from Exeter where he has been at the British Association. I ride with him on Hampton Common f. 6–8. It interests him very much as there is a camp on it and he thinks all the holes and mounds in it are ancient huts; he also finds several tumuli or long barrows.

Tues. 31 Aug. Augustus and I ride to Wheybury. I hold his horse while he walked over the field and found some flints which proved it to be a British camp, at all events pre-Roman. We also went inside a tumulus which had been opened up there; we had to crawl on our stomachs, there were several stone chambers inside. We went home through Woodchester Park . . .[13]

The quotation reveals the extent to which flints were associated with camps in Fox's mind, caused by the excavations at Cissbury. It will be appreciated how great was the surprise when a few years later the association turned out to be more apparent than real.

In the first six months of 1869 Fox went out from his home at Kensington to points up river where constructional work had revealed exposures of the Pleistocene gravel terraces of the river Thames (mainly at Acton). Since the recognition of the first handaxes in the Somme valley associated with the bones of extinct animals a few years before, this was regarded as a normal task for an archaeologist and Fox had done this elsewhere in England and on the Continent. In this case the results of his prolonged labours, suitably illustrated with sections and a map and with an identification of the fauna by George Busk, were given in a lecture to the Geological Society.[14]

Fox identified three terraces: high (with artefacts but no fauna), middle (fauna only) and low (with both). The sequence seemed to correspond with that known from the Somme and elsewhere at that time. The implements that were found are not illustrated in the article but are shown in the coloured drawings that exist at Salisbury. The sections that accompanied the lecture are geological sections of the period and it is evident that the experience he gained here influenced later excavation sections.

In October 1869 while staying with his wife's relatives at Penrhyn in north Wales, Fox opened two cairns about four miles south-east of Bangor.[15] One contained a cist and the other a pit with an urn. There are no plans or sections of the barrows and the excavator's comments on the urn are revealing of what he regarded as the real purpose of the excavation:

No two urns, however, hitherto discovered exactly resemble each other; and I have little doubt that if sufficient number of any given period could be brought together, it would be found that, like all other prehistoric remains, without exception, the several classes passed one into the other in such a manner that it would be impossible to draw any hard and fast line of separation between them. This is the normal characteristic of the products of all early and savage races, and should serve as a guide in classifying the relics of past ages where the evidence is doubtful or incomplete.

An abortive project of this period was a proposal of the British Association to excavate at Stonehenge[16] under the direction of Fox. He made it clear that the purpose of the excavation was simply to lift the turf to find objects to date the structure. His confidence in his ability to date objects is evidence of his belief in his series system. The owner would not agree and all things considered it was probably just as well.

It is time now to return to Canon Greenwell. In 1868 and 1869—the dates are not clear—Greenwell had cleared one of the shafts at Grimes Graves, near Brandon, in Norfolk. There are some 300 hollows in the Breckland, which we now know are the filled-in shafts of neolithic flint mines. The shafts, which are perhaps 15 ft in diameter and up to 40 ft deep with radiating galleries at the bottom, were dug to extract tabular flint that occurred at that level. Greenwell opened a shaft for the first time and his lecture on this in 1870,[17] a model of lucidity, is regarded by many as his best piece of work. Fox who was present praised the lecture and agreed with the interpretation. It must have been galling to him to know what he had missed at Cissbury.

So far as we know Fox did not excavate in 1871. In August 1872 he gave a lengthy address at the British Association, where Greenwell also spoke 'On Barrows of the Yorkshire Wolds.'[18] Greenwell's lecture aroused particular interest but the significant point is that before he returned to London Fox decided himself to open a barrow on Dyke Road, the Black Burgh Tumulas.[19] It contained a crouched skeleton accompanied by bronze dagger, bronze pin, food vessel and necklace of shale beads (a Wessex burial). There was material in the mound and secondary deposits. The main point however is that the recording with plan and section was of a much more careful kind than he had hitherto used on barrows. He also found holes in the chalk of a type mentioned by Greenwell in his lecture.

Pitt-Rivers' description of himself in later life as a pupil of Greenwell has sometimes been discounted but I am sure it is not so wide of the mark. Greenwell had a different attitude from the ordinary collector; he was assembling evidence on people who had left it in no other form. He perhaps helped to curb the slightly messianic streak in Fox. When Fox returned triumphantly to Cissbury in 1875 it was with the knowledge that Greenwell had provided him with at Grime's Graves. This was the key to his success and a turning point in his professional life.

Fox had been able to devote himself full time to his studies for six years. What had he achieved? He had gained very wide experience over a varied field and tried his hand at many things. He had shown a considerable organising ability in societies, but he was probably best known for his three lectures on primitive warfare. In excavation the results had been disappointing, for the desire to find objects to fit into series and sequences which overrode the need to study the structure of the sites he excavated had rendered the work unsatisfactory and unrewarding. The fact is, the two things did not mix and the decision first to lend and then to dispose of his collection freed him of an incubus which was impeding his efforts to master the techniques of excavation.

Early in 1873 Fox returned to full-time soldiering when he accepted command of a Brigade Depot at Guildford. The regular troops at the Depot consisted of the 1st and 2nd Battalions of West Surrey Regiment, the 2nd Regiment of Militia and Volunteers. They were presumably stationed in the formidable red-brick barracks in Stoughton Road, although the date of 1876 over the gateway suggests the buildings were still under construction while Fox was there. As the Post Office Directory reveals, he lived on the other side of the town in a house called Uplands, Merrow, on the northern edge of Merrow Downs.

This post carried the most responsibility of any that Fox held in his military career in which, of course, he could not advance unless he returned to full-time soldiering. It must have been irksome to leave London, but nevertheless with nine children (the last born in 1866) it must have been more economical, quite apart from the full pay to which he now reverted. There were therefore good career and economic reasons for taking the post.

His new responsibilities no doubt somewhat reduced the time he could devote to his studies but in one respect his new military authority allowed him to extend his interests into a new field, that of physical anthropology. He had 459 men and 18 officers of the 2nd Battalion of the Royal Surrey Militia measured according to the recommendations of the Anthropometric Committee of the British Association.[20] Note was taken of hair and eye colour, girth of chest, breathing-capacity and strength of arms. 92 per cent of the men came from within 20 miles of Guildford, and 81 per cent. were pure English. An interesting set of data was compiled although unfortunately there were no comparable figures with which to compare it, or at all events if there were he did not attempt to do so.

His promotion to Major-General was gazetted on October 1877 and the following year he returned to London. He spent the winter 1878–9 in France before establishing a permanent home at 19 Penywern Road, Earl's Court, where he lived for over a year. The road is lined by continuous terraces of four-storeyed houses (with attic and basement) with doorways flanked by Tuscan columns. The houses are now mainly rather seedy hotels although in the 1870s when they were new they were no doubt quite smart. When he came into the Cranborne Chase inheritance he returned to 4 Grosvenor Gardens, although he retained ownership of his former home until his death. There are few more telling indications of his changed circumstances than the move from Earl's Court to Belgravia.

In the 1870s Fox carried out some digging of barrows in the Guildford area which never reached full publication,[20] but in 1875 he began a series of excavations on Sussex hillforts that were entirely different in character from what he had done before. He knew what he was about and in a short time had built up a considerable body of information where hitherto there had been none.

The whole spirit and ethos of the work was quite different from that done later in Cranborne Chase. Financially the excavations were run on a shoestring, normally under the *aegis* of a society, a group of Fox's friends putting up the money. When the money ran out work stopped. The friends who had provided the finance also visited the excavation, and as from time to time Fox had to return to Guildford to carry out his military duties, someone had to stand in for him, usually his friend Rolleston. There was a spirit of camaraderie, sometimes almost reaching horseplay, in these undertakings that was absent from Cranborne Chase. In both paid labourers were employed to do the digging, but in the latter case the assistants were paid, while in the former they were friends.

This is a convenient point to introduce George Rolleston (1829–81). Slightly younger than Fox, he was a fellow Yorkshireman, having been born and bred at Maltby.[21] He graduated at Pembroke College, Oxford, and after qualifying at St Bartholomew's he practised as a doctor at Smyrna in 1853–57. He visited the siege of Sevastopol, another common experience with Fox. He had read the *Origin of Species* in January 1860 although he complained (like others) that the most cogent chapters came too late in the book. Like Lubbuck he had been present at the meeting of the British Association at Oxford when Huxley had made his famous retort to the Bishop of Oxford. He had been appointed to the Linacre Chair of Anatomy at Oxford in 1860. He was described by E. B. Tylor as 'richly endowed but diffuse'. He spent a great deal of time with Greenwell and was part author of his book on *British Barrows*. He accompanied Fox to the Continent in 1879 when they did some irregular digging on the Danewirke. Fox and he had planned to do some great study of domestic animals in Cranborne Chase, but Rolleston's untimely death in 1881 terminated what for Fox had been one of his closest friendships.

Cissbury hillfort stands on a hill to the north-east of Worthing. (4) It has a fine rampart and ditch which encloses in its western half a number of hollows (now largely overgrown) which occur also outside the defences on the south-west. When Fox dug there in 1867–8 flint mines had not been heard of but since then they had come to light at Spiennes in Belgium, while Greenwell had opened the shaft at Grimes' Graves. (If you know what you are looking for in excavation, as in many other things, you are more likely to find it.) In April Fox was at Cissbury working on his own with five men and from June to September with 5–10 men on behalf of a Committee of the Anthropological Institute. At a conversazione of the Royal Society he had proposed the formation of such a Committee and raised '30± which will probably suffice to complete the necessary examination'. He had many visitors from the Anthropological Institute, some of whom participated in the work.[22]

If the hollows were flint mines then at the point where the bank and ditch had hollows both inside and out, it should be possible to demonstrate which impinged on which and so which was later. At the point Fox chose to test this there could be no doubt that the ditch had been dug through the white chalky filling of the shaft of a flint mine. By following the shaft down to the radiating galleries at the bottom he was able to satisfy himself that it was indeed a flint mine of the type revealed by Greenwell at Grimes' Graves. It was quite evident that two entirely different monuments occurred at Cissbury: neolithic (Greenwell's dating at Grimes' Graves) flint mines and a defensive earthwork of a much later date.

For the first time at Cissbury Fox dug 'sections'. These are such a commonplace of archaeology today that one forgets that they had to be invented. The principle is very simple; a trench at right angles to the line of bank cuts through the bank and ditch and is taken down to solid chalk. Everything underfoot is a geological deposit, while the sides of the trenches represent the depth of modern non-geological material in the case of the bank and natural silting in the case of the ditch.

As Fox's understanding of the deposits grew so his grasp of the purpose of the sections became clearer, as we can see by comparing the last section with the earlier ones. In the latter case the rampart in sequence of construction consisted of: (1) surface earth, (2) chalk embankment and (3) an addition of successive layers of turf and rubble. All objects in the rampart must be older than it. 25 sherds of pottery, red or black, which differed from the sherds in the shaft filling, were found in it. If some kind of date could be attached to the sherds then Fox would be able to date both monuments, flint mine and hillfort. A great vertical section was left open for geologists to be able to study the work while a model of the section was completed for display with his collection in the Bethnal Green Museum. As we have seen, Fox had met models at Sandhurst and the Royal United Service Institution and no doubt elsewhere in service life. This was the first of the models that were to become such a feature of the excavations in Cranborne Chase.

For Fox the 1875 season at Cissbury was like the conversion of St Paul. Excavation, instead of being primarily a search for objects to arrange in series, had become a field of endeavour in its own right. Significant information could be obtained from it both about a monument and about its relationship to others. This after all is the crucial point about digging. You can dig to look for objects, the usual motive for early barrow-digging, or you can dig to disencumber foundations to reveal the plan of a building. In both these cases the soil is a nuisance to be disposed of as quickly as possible, but what Fox was doing was to interpret the history of the site from the way the deposition of soils and stone had taken place. The white chalky fill of the flint shaft was different from the silt in the ditch, while the rampart was not of course a natural silting but a sudden creation by human agency. Objects in these matrices had a different relationship to the monument. Clearly in this type of work, although the digger needed to find objects in his deposits to make inferences about the history of the monument, this was secondary to understanding the processes of formation of the deposits.

Although as we have seen Fox was used to looking at Pleistocene gravel sections and to interpreting them in terms of fauna and fossils he was not, I think, influenced to any high degree at Cissbury by this. Otherwise we might have expected his published sections to have looked like geological sections but they are in fact decidedly sketchy. He seems to have been guided simply by common sense—there ought to be a shaft here, it ought to look like what Greenwell found, all this bank must have been thrown up at once. No doubt, of course, his gravel-pit experience made the idea of vertical sections and pottery sherds serving as fossils less strange than it might otherwise have been (at an unconscious level one might say). Undoubtedly more important was his three-dimensional grasp of the site that presumably derives from the military surveying for fortification of which we have spoken. He always used a spirit-level for making a surface section, as can be seen in the published drawing from the 1860s at Roovesmore and even more clearly in the Inspector's notebooks discussed in the next chapter. It is fairly clear from the published figures that he saw the excavated sections as elaborations or extensions of these surface-measurements rather than as separate creations of their own.

For Fox 1875 was an *annus mirabilis*. It saw the culmination and termination of his studies on the 'Evolution of Culture' in the lecture to the Royal Institution. Apart from the excitement at Cissbury, a number of visitors to the site and assistants were Fellows of the Royal Society who were to be his sponsors for election to Fellowship in the next winter.

No doubt his duties at Guildford hindered his freedom to dig although he had a season at Seaford in 1876. In September, 1877 when his promotion to Major-General was about to be gazetted he dug at Mount Caburn hillfort, near Lewes, until October and the next year at Caesar's Camp, Folkestone (very near the School of Musketry at Hythe) 3 June–5 July 1878, returning to Mount Caburn for a second campaign in the same month.

Mount Caburn hillfort is situated on a steeper hill than Cissbury, so that the centre of the camp is a domed hill top; at the entry on the col side the defences are formidable but much slighter on the steep hillside. There is another camp slightly to the west, Ranscombe, where Fox also dug. He was able to make considerable advance in the study of the structures.[23] Small pits about 3 ft in diameter and 2–5 ft deep were revealed. These are the well-known 'storage pits' we associate with Iron Age occupation. He concluded that they were not graves, or habitations but could not decide on a purpose. Just as interesting was evidence for the use of timber in the defences, postholes at the front of the inner rampart and some kind of revetment in the outer (?earlier) rampart. A section at Ranscombe camp revealed Roman pottery in the upper level of the ditch, but he concluded the camp itself was earlier than Mount Caburn.

He was lucky enough to find five British coins which at once gave a firm date to the occupation of the camp in the last century B.C. or first century A.D. Slingstones came to light, while spindle whorls and weaving combs indicated cloth-making. There were iron objects including a knife-handle ornamented with dot-and-circle pattern, a 'bastard survival of the great period of spiral ornaments.' Three types of pottery, the finest being smooth and sometimes decorated, were defined. For the first time Fox used 'Relic Tables', lists of finds with place and date of discovery. From originals which survive in the papers at Salisbury the full process of how he arrived at these can be studied.[23a]

It was a remarkable achievement to have placed the camp within an historical context, or more accurately in a prehistoric context just before the beginning of the historic period. No doubt it could be reasonably inferred from Julius Caesar's account that the work was likely to be of that period but it was quite a different matter to demonstrate that it was so. It is not surprising that the discussion at the Society of Antiquaries after his lecture on 20 June 1878 caused him to return there after he had finished at Caesar's Camp where he was then digging.

Caesar's Camp, entirely misnamed as it turned out, differed from Cissbury or Mount Caburn in that it was not a simple enclosure but a double one, an inner citadel within a larger enclosure.[24] Fox described his method of excavation as that used in other camps:

to cut several sections through the ditches and ramparts and observe what relics might be found on the line of the old surface, beneath the rampart and in the bottoms of the ditches, to excavate the pits as far as the undisturbed sides and bottom, . . . to cut trenches in the interior to ascertain whether habitations could be discovered and to compare the sherds of pottery in the interior with those found beneath the rampart. . . .'[25]

Work had started off with sappers from Shorncliffe but continued with a team of 8–10 men.

Some of Fox's aphorisms have passed into the lore of archaeology, as one that he used here: 'In order that the evidence obtained may be strictly reliable, it should, if possible, be of a character that might be accepted in a court of justice.'[25] (The phrase takes on a different emphasis when we know he acted as prosecuting officer at courts martial in Ireland).

It was soon apparent that the earthwork was very different from Cissbury and Mount Caburn. A silver penny of King Stephen, a socketed arrowhead, a small copper-gilt object were found. Most of the pottery found in the bank was of sandy texture (what we should call medieval cooking pottery) although there was green glazed sherds as well. There were also horseshoes with sinuous edges. Everything indeed that we would now regard as standard twelfth-century remains was listed in the relic tables.

Many earthworks of this kind usually with a motte or donjon are known from France. As Fox said although it was unwalled there was no reason for doubting its Norman date. 'Having brought the Camp within the pale of historic times, I leave later speculation on the subject to historians.' Historians did indeed speculate on it 30 years later.

The subject is of some interest. At the time Fox was writing the generally accepted theory, or at all events the view of the leading authority on the subject, George T. Clark, was that mottes and associated earthworks were of Late Saxon origin, that they were Saxon Burhs. This was the view adopted by Clark in his two-volume work

Medieval Military Architecture published in 1884. The only reason for adopting this opinion was the difficulty of believing that the Normans could ever have built in anything but stone. This view was overthrown in the early years of this century by the joint efforts of three scholars: Horace Round, St John Hope and Ella Armitage. Since then it has been accepted as read that earthen castles were virtually unknown before the Norman Conquest but were the normal form immediately afterwards. Round was a historian and so was unlikely to be influenced by evidence of the kind offered by Fox, but it certainly played some part in the thinking of Hope and Mrs Armitage, both archaeologists. In this matter then Fox was ahead of his time.

In three brief years Fox had identified and dated three major types of earthwork on the Sussex Downs: neolithic flint mines, iron-age hillforts and Norman castles. In many ways it was the most impressive achievement of his career. More important than this, he had demonstrated that those somewhat unpromising earthworks could be made to yield a great deal of information about themselves if tackled in the right way, using his sectional methods. They were not dumb witnesses but on some matters could be made to speak, although it was clearly a laborious and expensive business to make them do so.

Three other excavations that Fox undertook before the move to Cranborne Chase deserve brief mention. At Sigwell, near Compton, Somerset he excavated a twin barrow and a single barrow in close association with Professor Rolleston.[26] Indeed the latter seems largely to have directed the work while Fox went scouting in the neighbourhood. The plan is contoured, something to which he attached great weight later. The southern mound produced a bark coffin containing burnt bones and a bronze dagger.

Rolleston and Fox paid a visit together to Denmark in 1879 to look at museums and while in the area made a small excavation in the Danewirke in Schleswig.[27] They found evidence of timber in the earthwork, but this is only known from a casual reference.

Probably connected with this was an excavation he made on Dane's Dyke in the East Riding of Yorkshire in October, 1879. This massive earthwork that cuts off Flamborough Head had been seen by him when he had been in the East Riding with Canon Greenwell in 1867. Owing to the size of the bank he used a system of boxes, filling a lower box as he dug one higher and so on, instead of a continuous trench. He had been warned by friends that the work was not likely to be worthwhile and he in fact found no evidence for dating the earthwork. The nugatory result is perhaps mainly of interest in that it must have impressed upon his mind that with linear earthworks it is necessary to chose a point for sectioning where it is known that there are remains of certain date adjoining—in order to relate them. This was to prove the key to the understanding of the dykes in Cranborne Chase.

VI
PROTECTION OF MONUMENTS

As we have seen, by comparing the raths shown on the Ordnance Survey sheets for Munster (about 10,000) with what was visible on the ground, Fox had become aware of the high rate of destruction. The problem remained in his mind, but it was only when he became closely associated with Sir John Lubbock that it became possible to think of practical measures to remedy the situation. Before turning to Lubbock there is yet a further point to be made about Ireland.

On the disestablishment of the Irish Church in 1869 a considerable body of ecclesiastical ruins were transferred to the care of the Board of Works in Ireland. It was clear that there was no law of nature preventing the Government from taking monuments into its care and the Irish precedent was to be quoted in Parliament in the 1870s in the debates on Lubbock's Bill. The Irish precedent also meant that if there was Government legislation it was reasonably certain that the First Commissioner of Works would be responsible for implementing it.

In 1865 at the time of the publication of *Prehistoric Times* Lubbock was contesting a Parliamentary seat, unsuccessfully as it turned out for he was not elected until 1870. In the book Lubbock had rudimentary ideas about protection, prompted by damage at Avebury, and by what he had recently seen in Denmark where he had been to study the kitchen middens:

... well worthy of consideration whether Government would not act wisely in selecting some competent archaeologist, who might be appointed Conservator of National Antiquities; whose duty it would be to preserve, as far as possible, from wanton injury, the graves of our ancestors, and other interesting memorials of the past; to make careful drawings of all those which have not yet been figured. ... The Danish Government have bought for the nation a large number of tumuli. . . .[1]

In view of how Pitt-Rivers later actually carried out his duties the reference to the Conservator of National Antiquities is pregnant with interest. The Scandinavian origin of Lubbock's ideas is also interesting.

If Lubbock and Fox were acquainted by the mid-1860s (p. 32) the first evidence we have of them actually acting in concert on the question of protection was at the International Congress on Prehistoric Archaeology at Norwich in August, 1868, a point of re-direction in so many other ways for Fox. A letter from the Rev. W. C. Lukis had drawn attention to the destruction of megalithic monuments in Brittany. A Committee was set up to arrest, if possible, the destruction, consisting of Lubbock, Evans, Flower, Fox and Lukis.[2] Lubbock was President of the Organising Committee as we have seen, and Fox Secretary, so they had close dealings on many other matters. From this time on both men were involved in protection more or less for the rest of their lives, Fox probably more than Lubbock.

Both the reconstituted Ethnological Society and the Society of Antiquaries became caught up in threats to monuments. Fox himself acted as an emissary, visiting sites, remonstrating with owners and even in one case, Dorchester-on-Thames,[3] carrying out a survey to measure the degree of destruction taking place. He had become a sort of self-appointed Inspector of Ancient Monuments.

A Committee of the Ethnological Society had been 'formed for the purpose of describing and preserving the Prehistoric Monuments of Great Britain and Ireland.' So Fox wrote on 20 July 1870 to Professor Worsaae in Copenhagen[3a] on behalf of the Council, asking 'particularly in regard to powers assumed by the Government of your Country in preserving those monuments which are the private property of individuals and which are threatened with destruction by their owners.' Lubbock had been Secretary and President and was then a Vice-President of the Society; no document could illustrate more clearly how closely Fox was associated with the project and the extent to which they were both influenced by the Scandinavian example.

Fox's enthusiasm was not shared by all his fellow antiquaries, and as it became evident in the early 1870s that legislation would be a long haul, Fox turned increasingly bitter about the lack of support. Speaking of the Bill at the British Association at Brighton in 1872 he said:

The first enquiry has been as to which of these societies has had the credit of having originated the measure, and if found to be tainted by the support of a rival society, it has at once been repudiated.[4]

Lubbock entered Parliament in 1870 as a Liberal. Although he was on friendly terms with Gladstone he never held office and his varied reforms were introduced as private Bills. To the surprise of many his Bank Holiday Bill was passed quickly and turned him into something of a national hero. His Early Closing Bill and Ancient Monuments Bill touched more sensitive areas and took many years to reach the Statute Book. Lubbock re-introduced the Bill, slightly modified, at each session, each time pushing it farther forward. Although the Hansard debates are fascinating reading it would be tedious to follow the Bill's history. By 1879 it had reached the Lords and it was thought that the battle was won. In fact it was referred to a Committee with the knowledge that the impending dissolution would kill it. At the election Lubbock lost his seat and it was a short while before he returned as the member for London University. He felt now that it was incumbent upon the Government to introduce a Bill. They did so in a form considerably modified from Lubbock's and this became the Ancient Monuments Act in October, 1882.

The main objection to the Bill by its opponents was that it interfered with the rights of private property. This was of course a very sensitive area in Victorian England, but there are two aspects of this to be considered. Lubbock saw protection as a fairly crude transference of the monuments in question to a body acting in the name of the State. Had he been able to devise some formula by which the owner retained the title but was restricted as to use (like modern scheduling) he might have been able to take the wind out of the sails of the opposition.

When Lubbock had stood unsuccessfully for Parliament in 1865 his agent had advised him to delay the publication of *Prehistoric Times* as it would cost him votes. He refused and his opponent was returned with an increased majority.[5] Views that were controversial in the 1860s were hardly so in 1870, but nevertheless a residual distrust remained. Lubbock was a regular churchgoer (except for 'one short interval of insistent scepticism') and neither he nor Fox were self-proclaimed agnostics like Huxley. Nevertheless both had been closely associated with what the old-fashioned regarded as views hostile to the social order.

What made the matter more curious was that protection was to be confined to prehistoric monuments. It was argued by Lubbock that as no conservation was involved the cost of taking prehistoric monuments into state care was negligible, a cogent argument in that period. Nevertheless there were those who favoured protection but could not support the Bill on the grounds that it did not go far enough. It was indeed an extraordinary situation that in a Christian country only the pagan monuments should be protected, on the grounds of economy. The fact is, of course, Lubbock attached special weight to prehistoric monuments. Fox put the matter thus in 1870:

The historic monument is interesting as a means of realizing the information which history conveys to us; but the prehistoric monument assumes double importance from its affording the only available evidence of the period to which it belongs. Judging by the rapid progress which prehistoric archaeology has made during the last ten years ... nothing compared to what is stored up ... and the duty of handing them down intact for the more enlightened judgement of posterity is one which the Government of a civilised country will do ill to neglect.'[6]

The objections to the Bill, then, were partly that it infringed the rights of private property, and partly opposition to the people who supported it. Nothing is more revealing about the nature of the opposition to it than the concessions that had to be made so that the Bill could reach the statute book. From an independent commission (of which Fox was named as a member) the duties of implementation were shifted to the

Trustees of the British Museum. In the Government Bill there was no outside body and the responsible minister was the First Commissioner of Works although with the important provision of an Inspector to advise him. There were no compulsory powers in the Act which allowed the Commissioners to take into their care such of the 64 prehistoric monuments listed at the end as the owners might wish to offer. It has been described as 'permissive' and may perhaps be regarded more as a declaration of intent rather than a serious legislative measure.

During the whole of this decade, 1870–80, Fox was standing in the wings so to speak waiting for legislation that required implementation in the field. It was clear that he would be associated with this in some way and indeed that when it came to 'belling the cat' he would find scarcely any rivals. Evidence that Fox was schooling himself for this role was published by the present writer a few years ago. It consisted of two sketchbooks that Fox had taken with him on journeys made to Brittany in the Autumn (October–November) of 1878 and in the Spring (March–April) of 1879.[7] He spent the intervening winter in France. He had not shown much interest in megaliths before this date, but at this time of course it really looked as if Lubbock's Bill would become law and the main class of monuments affected by it would have been megaliths.

On the first journey the time was mainly spent in the classic megalithic area around Carnac, with a short time in the north; while in the second year the journey started in the north, moving south near Carnac and then in Finisterre. He was evidently travelling by himself so did not have assistance with the record which is his own. He normally therefore confined himself to a plan and drawing of which one of the better examples is shown in (5) with the sketchbook opened to show the plan on one side and the sketch on the other. The human figure acting as scale was a normal feature of Fox's drawings.

Some of the principal monuments dealt with in the books are Gavrinis, Pierres Plates, Table des Marchands, Mané Lud, Kerhuen Tangui, Keriaval in 1878 and Bois du Rocher nr. Pleudihan, Allée Couverte at Genilan, Pierre Sonnante and castle of Le Guildo, objects found in dolmens, various church details, Camp D'Artus, Church of Sept Saints at Plouaret, churches of Notre Dame de Bon Secour, and St Leonard, and so on, in 1879. There are a surprising number of churches and also various objects. He seems indeed to have grown tired of dolmens! These two notebooks were given to the Office of Works in the 1920s together with the books recording his journeys as official inspector. In these the record is basically similar but becomes more elaborate in order to provide the record to make a model of the monument. He did not normally go around making such an elaborate record and so the question is at once prompted, why did he do so on these journeys?

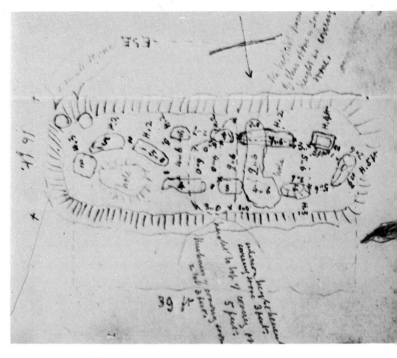

5 Plan and sketch by Pitt-Rivers of megalith at
Bois des Rochers, Pleudihan, Brittany.

Lubbock in 1865 had said that one of the functions of the Conservator of National Antiquities should be to record monuments (p. 58). In the Commons' debates a frequent analogy was made with Historical Manuscripts Commission implying that recording was almost as important as protection in the proposed legislation. Fox certainly attached very great weight to this side of the work, although as the results were never published few people are aware of the pains he took.

But the rapid growth of our administrative services is on the whole due less to headquarters than to the Inspectorate. Inspection was in the air: the Factory Inspectors of 1834 were followed by the Prison Inspectors, and these by School Inspectors, the Railways Inspectors and the Mine Inspectors. The Inspectors, like higher officials, were often men of mature experience who came to their duties with ideas already formed.[8]

G. M. Young was speaking of mid-Victorian England but it still held in the last decades of the Queen's reign. Where today a Board or Committee would be appointed the individualistic Victorian solution was an Inspector. For this reason the Inspector has lost status in the Govern-

view from the north.

ment machine since that time. In the nineteenth century it was a covetted honour, and indeed the way the information was conveyed to Pitt-Rivers by Lord Stalbridge[9] was done almost as if his name was to appear in the Honours List. One thinks of Mathew Arnold or perhaps more appositely of Thomas Huxley, who was appointed Inspector of Fisheries at about the same time as Pitt-Rivers became Inspector of Ancient Monuments.

The purpose of appointing an eminent man as Inspector was to overawe the dissidents, confound them with his knowledge and give Government action that extra authority that the situation required. Both sides gained kudos from the appointment. In the case of ancient monuments the debates in Parliament had shown that rights of private property were the main problem, and it was clearly inherently easier for a man who owned 25,000 acres to speak to other landowners on equal terms. Given the social conditions of Victorian society it was evident that the enforcement of any legislation that caused officials to enter on to private estates would have been a formidable problem.

Before discussing the activities of Pitt-Rivers as Inspector it would be useful to consider how he saw himself in this role. What was the relationship between this post and the excavations in Cranborne Chase?

We may refer here to Eugène Emmanuel Viollet-le-Duc (1814–79), an architect with the official title of Inspector concerned with the restoration of historic buildings in France, who published his famous ten-volume *Dictionnaire raisonné de l'architecture francaise* (1854–68) and six-volume *Dictionnaire raisonné du mobilier francais* (1858–75). His memory dominates medieval architectural studies in France today as does that of Pitt-Rivers in field archaeology in this country. Although of course he worked in quite a different field Pitt-Rivers was certainly aware of the activities of the great Inspecteur-General. Lubbock suggested to Pitt-Rivers that he might fill the post in October, 1882 and he received an invitation in November; he was trying to buy a copy of Viollet-le-Duc's work only a few weeks later.[9a] It was clearly an example that profoundly influenced him.

Having spent all his life in the army he was accustomed to a title that gave him authority. While the excavations had been started before he was appointed Inspector and were entirely financed out of his own pocket, yet the title threw a faint aura of officialdom over them. Some people indeed thought that they were officially inspired. There is a hint of this again in the great volumes in which the results were recorded, printed as they were by Harrison & Son, Printers in Ordinary to Her Majesty. No doubt Pitt-Rivers would have carried out excavations whether he had had the title or not but its conferment in a subtle way influenced their character.

When the Government Bill was in gestation in February 1882 Lubbock had raised the question of Inspectors,[10] and he raised the matter with Pitt-Rivers in October so that the invitation in November evidently did not come as a surprise. Pitt-Rivers took up his duties on 1 January 1883; the period of the Inspectorship falls into two quite distinct parts: 1883–90 when he received a salary of £250 a year and 1890 to his death in 1900 when the post was an honorary one. In the first part he carried out the journeys that will be the subject of the rest of this chapter.

What exactly were the Inspector's duties? They were decidedly limited. At the end of the Act was a list of 50 monuments in England, Scotland and Wales, and 14 others in Ireland dealt with separately by the Irish Board of Works. The owners could offer these into state care (there was no compulsion) and additions could be made to the Schedule as it was called. At the death of Pitt-Rivers 26 of the original monuments on the schedule and 17 additional ones had been 'registered', to use his expression, that is the owner had entered into a deed of guardianship with the Commissioners of Works.[10a]

There was a tense period when Pitt-Rivers was first appointed since it looked as if no owners would offer up their monuments.[11] Even Lub-

Within the sketch:
Wood of Pins and for trees
Corn field
Stone wall
Roadway
View from the South East

6 Sketch by Tomkin of un-named chambered tomb
with figure of Pitt-Rivers acting as scale

bock hesitated over Silbury Hill since it was thought that such an arrangement would depreciate the value of the land. It shows him in a somewhat unfavourable light. The impasse was broken by Sir Herbert Maxwell, who came forward to offer his own monuments and persuaded others to do likewise. Thus Pitt-Rivers began his journeys to visit the owners and monuments.

The 14 notebooks and sketchbooks that record the journeys in 1883–90 are among the most rewarding documents that have survived from his life. I have discussed them in detail elsewhere.[12] Four of the 14 are in the hand of Pitt-Rivers himself and the others by his assistants, mainly Tomkin. Pitt-Rivers travelled alone in 1883, with Tomkin in 1884–7 and with two or three assistants in 1887–90. The record consists of plan and section in the notebooks and sketches in the sketchbook. There may be then a single, double, triple or quadruple record in one year, so the Editor's problem was to work out the full record for each year (apart of course from the difficulties of deciphering the pencil entries written in the open air in a book only supported in the hand) but once this was done by myself the books became usable.

First interest must of course attach to the record of the monuments that he visited. This usually consists of plan, section and sketch. The noteworthy point is that they are not seen redrawn and reduced for

Sun in background

Beach tree

Slope

PATH

Slope

View from South

7 Sketch of Wayland's Smithy by Tomkin, with Pitt-Rivers acting as scale

publication but actually as they were recorded in the field. Almost as fascinating are the notes of travelling expenses, lists of purchases, comments on hotels, the diary kept by Tomkin and so on. Before dealing with some of these matters we should briefly run through where Pitt-Rivers went each year:

1883. Starting in April Kit's Coty House in Kent, West Kennett, Silbury; Earl's Barton, Rollright stones, Danes' Camp; monuments in south-west area (Stoney Littleton, Nymphsfield, Uley). From 29 August to 9 September various monuments on the way to Scotland: Nine Ladies, Minning Low, Arborlow, Mayborough, Arthur's Round Table etc. The visit to Scotland, usually with his wife, now became a normal event. In this year he travelled alone.

1884. This year he was accompanied by Tomkin using the sketchbook. He went to the Midlands and Wales (Arthur's Quoit, Pentre Ifan) in the early summer, and in the late summer the east coast of Scotland (crosses at St Vigean's church, Black and White Cathertuns, Aberlemno crosses, Bass of Inverurie, Clava tombs etc.).

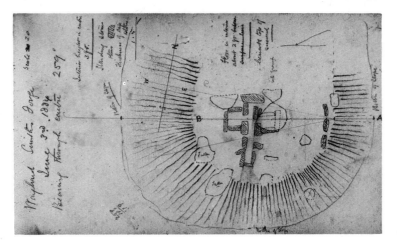

8 Plan of Wayland's Smithy by Tomkin

9 Section of Wayland's Smithy by Pitt-Rivers

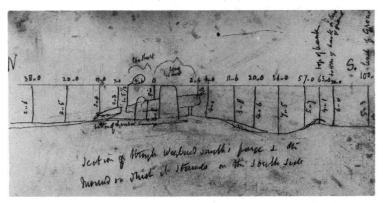

1885. The 50 monuments on the schedule had probably all been dealt with by now. Pitt-Rivers, accompanied by his wife and Tomkin, left London on 27 July on what was perhaps the most ambitious and interesting journey of all. Dropping off in Cumberland and Westmorland for two or three prehistoric monuments they moved up the west coast of Scotland, then to the Orkney islands. A few of the many sites visited that may be mentioned are Callernish stones, broch of Carloway, Ring of Brogar, shielings at Morsgail in Lewis and so on.

1886. There are some sketches done in October: Moat of Urr,

crosses at Whithorn and St Ninian's Cave and so on. Scottish crosses—of which he had a number of models made—became his main interest in the later 1880s.[13] In December, North Wales.

1888. One of the notebooks records expenses for a journey into South Wales (one first-class and two third-class tickets, indicating that Pitt-Rivers was travelling with two assistants). An increasing amount of museum material now features in the notebooks.

1889. In this year the notebooks record many sections made by Tomkin at Yarnbury Castle and Wansdyke, a reminder that the same staff went on the journeys who had done the excavations in Cranborne Chase.[14] According to the late H. St George Gray the same type of field notebook with metal clasp was used in recording the excavations as was used on the journeys.

On 27 July Pitt-Rivers, Tomkin and C. W. Gray (the elder brother of H. St George Gray) set out for Scotland but Pitt-Rivers was recalled to London on 1 August. The two assistants worked alone until he rejoined them on the twenty-ninth of the month. The main object of the journey was clearly to draw early Christian crosses, but work was done on Hadrian's wall on the return journey.

1890. Two journeys by assistants to register monuments, take measurements for models, look into questions of public access and so on, South Wales and Cotswolds.

In recording a basically similar method was used to that employed in Brittany. In 1883 Pitt-Rivers confined himself to plans and sections but in 1884–5 he had Tomkin to do the sketches. The interesting point is that as Tomkin did the sketch he had Pitt-Rivers before him doing the plan, and in at least four instances he has clearly drawn in Pitt-Rivers himself (6, 7) to serve as scale. They give a charming glimpse of the subject of our essay actually at work in the field.

Sketching was an extremely simple way of recording because it required so little equipment and of course had been familiar to Pitt-Rivers since Sandhurst days. Photography had been known from the middle of the nineteenth century but a plate camera, tripod and plates were a cumbersome load in this type of work. In 1889 considerable practice in photography was undertaken and in that summer a camera was taken to Scotland. So in the first decade of Cranborne Chase (volumes i–iii contain no photographs but there are several in volume iv) a camera was not used, but it was in the second.

The load of equipment taken on these journeys was considerable as the following quotation shows:

Instruments taken to Scotland with General Pitt-Rivers, July, 1889: Tapes two 100 ft and 1 50 ft, levelling rod in case, walking stick levelling rod, pocket level, field glass, Prismatic compass, clinometer, Camera lucida, Camera table and seat, Set of Ivory scales, Sketch block, Military sketch book, Watercolours brushes etc., Aneroid, Pocket compasses, White cards with ruled border,

Protractor, Plummet, Tape (small), Pencils, Blotting paper, notepaper, foolscap etc., labels.

Photographic apparatus comprising: Leather case containing camera, lens, tripod top screw, cases of stops, three dark slides, Focussing cloth, Tripod (this can generally be strapped and carried with levelling staff etc.).

Guide books etc.: Murray's, Black's, Baddeleys map of Scotland in two parts, envelopes containing traces of the following crosses and instruments... (there follows a long list of sites, offprints, numbers of journals) two rolls of Ordnance Maps. 20 copies of Ancient Monuments Act, 25 copies of 'Committee of Ard,' box containing five plate boxes for dry plates with straps... two volumes (in brown paper cover) *The Orkneys and Shetland, Arch. Scotia* Vol. 5, *Clickanim*.

All this equipment, in addition to personal luggage, was taken by train, so the travelling must have been a truly formidable operation. From the hotel to site travel was by fly. A quotation from the travelling expenses of Pitt-Rivers will illustrate how he travelled by himself in 1883. The £1 that he puts down each night is what he could claim from the Office of Works in subsistence:

August 29, 1883

		£	s.	d.
Aug. 29	Cab to station		2	0
Aug. 29	London 1st class to Bakewell	1	0	0
Aug. 29	Night at Bakewell	1	0	0
Aug. 30	To Rowsley and back		2	0
	Fly to Hob's Hurst House,			
	1 day, futile attempt	1	4	0
Aug. 30	1 night at Bakewell	1	0	0
Aug. 31	Bakewell to Rowsley and back		2	0
Aug. 31	Fly one day, two horses Rowsley to			
	Nine Ladies, Minning Low	2	0	0
Sept. 1	Fly to Arbelow to Mr. Sleigh			
	and Mr. Hesfield, Duke of			
	Rutland's agent	1	10	0

Tomkin kept a diary for parts of some of the journeys. This abbreviated extract made on one of the most ambitious of the Scottish journeys in 1885 gives a vivid glimpse of work in progress. He was a young man and evidently excited by the journey.

July 27th. '85. Monday.
Left London from Euston at 10 o'clock, arrived at Keswick about 6.45....
Tuesday, July 28th.
Left Keswick by train at 8.15 for Whitehaven.... Went to Devil's Circle and made sketch and took section.... at Whitehaven had to wait there an hour, so walked on to pier and saw an iron ship building....
Left Keswick on Wednesday at 9.45 for Penrith.... Drove to Shap Abbey

from there to circle (double) of stones near Gunnerskeld Farm about 3 miles from Shap. Made coloured sketch whilst General made plan. Afterwards made sketch . . . Before leaving Shap visited the remains of stone circle near L. and N.W. Railway, portion of which was destroyed or covered in constructing the line. . . .

July 30th. Thursday.

Leave today for Farnboro'. . . . Had a pleasant journey riding 1st. class train being full. . . .

Friday July 31st.

Working out sections and plans and finishing water color sketches, all day indoors. In the evening went into Scottish Academy. . . .

Saturday August 1st.

Leave by 11.30 train for Castle Cary near Falkirk. Made sections etc. of remains of Roman Wall. . . .

Tuesday Aug 4th.

. . . Drove to Serpentine Mound near Oban, took sketch, plan and section thro' same. . . . In the evening went round the sea shore to Dunolly Castle. Had a splendid view of Ben Cruachan.

Wednesday August 5th.

. . . Went into Fingal's Cave and round causeway to top of island. From there to Iona. Did not go to cathedral or cross but made sketch of stone (tomb) in Nunnery of Princess Anna.

Friday August 7th.

Stayed in during morning, worked at sections etc. In afternoon went to take plan etc. of shieling near Gairloch. . . .

Monday August 10th.

Drove to Callernish stones. Made water colour sketch of same, also began plan. . . .

Wednesday August 12th.

Drove with General and Mrs. R. and W. and Mrs. Tylor to Barras. Visited large standing stone from there, also some cottages, and in evening went to see Flora Macdonald (an old woman) make some pottery with blue clay. . . .

Thursday August 13th.

Left Barras at 8.30 driving to Carloway, on the way sketching and making plans of two horse mills and a brook near road. Went on to Pictish Tower at Carloway and made water colour sketch whilst General took plan etc. From there drove to Callernish and whilst others went up to see the stones I went and inspected small circle of stones standing near Gary-na-hine Inn. . . .

Friday August 14th.

Drove to Loch Morsgail (Morsgail shooting lodge) to see Beehive house Scenery very wild here. Changed horses at Gary-na-hine Inn. . . .

Monday August 17th.

Left Stornaway at 3 o'clock a.m. for Strome Ferry and had a very fair passage across the Minch, the water being very smooth. The morning light in the distant hills was very fine, the air very cold. . . .

Tuesday August 18th.

Stayed in all day working out drawings of horse mills and shielings etc. taken in Lewis.

Wednesday August 19th.

Working indoors all day. . . .
Friday 21st.
Got up at 5.30 and had a walk before breakfast to 'Cat's Back.'
Saturday 22nd.
Went to see vitrified forest on Scuir Marksie near the falls of Corion. Very hot day. Took plan and sketch of hill. . . .
Monday 24th.
. . . In afternoon went to Dingwall with the General and accompanied by Mr. Joass (architect) drove to see some cup stones etc. . . .
Wednesday 26th.
Working indoors all morning. In afternoon went with General to take plan and sketches of group of stones on the end of 'Cat's Back' near the village of Jamestown. . . .
Friday 28th.
Went with General and Mrs. R. and Dr. Joass of Golspie to Dunrobin to see museum etc. etc. Afterwards drove to remains of Pictish Tower then to 2 or 3 others in woods above Dunrobin C. . . .
Saturday 29th.
Drove to Stennis, took sketches etc. of standing stones and visited 'Maeshowe'. . . .
Sunday 30th. August
Drove out in afternoon with General and Mrs. R. to see some corn drying kilns etc. Took plans etc. of same. Went into the Cathedral (St. Magnus) to make sketches of old tomb stones with iron shod spades.

In this and the previous two chapters I have described how cultural evolution, fieldwork and protection had been the three subjects of interest to Pitt-Rivers since the 1860s. In the Inspector's notebooks the three are interwoven in a manner that displays these interests in a quite remarkable way. The journeys were undertaken for protection, the record is an example of fieldwork and the interest in folk culture and the purchases are indications of his continuing interest in cultural evolution.

In Brittany in 1879 there is a note of "Amber beads" ("pateulette"), an uneven number are worn round the neck. . . . to cure sore throats . . .', while beneath a fine drawing of a church Pitt-Rivers unexpectedly writes: 'Church of St Leonard, Guingamp, where the snails are used as a cure for fever.' Unusual types of agricultural implements especially caught his attention; it will be recalled that he formed a collection of these at Farnham. There are several drawings of carts and ploughs in Brittany and sledges, turf-cutting implements, horsemills and so on in Scotland. Crofting and shielings were of special interest to him.

Pitt-Rivers was also purchasing items as he moved around. A nutcracker is illustrated in the Breton notebooks, while at Penrith in 1883 he bought 'a pair of wooden soled boots used by the country people, 6 shillings.' The following is an example of such a list of purchases made in 1885:

Bought of George Sim, naturalist, 14, King St., Aberdeen:

	£	s	d
1 stone ball, Parish of Fyvie, Aberdeen	1	5	0
1 stone cup	1	10	0
Bronze brooch		15	0
1 gold brooch, harp (shape)		5	0
5 silver small [brooches]		13	9
5 flint arrowheads		19	0
1 iron [?] bound spade for turning cakes		2	0
1 Poor Man's candlestick		15	0
1 Poor Man's jointed [candlestick]	1	0	0
1 Irish bagpipe	1	5	0
2 4ft. iron arrowhead anvils		9	0
3 spindle whorls		5	0
1 sporran? kilt	1	10	0
	10	17	0[sic]

The books contain other interesting material, evidently jottings made when a thought crossed his mind. We may refer to two. Pitt-Rivers was the owner of the chalk-cut figure at Cerne Abbas, Dorset, known as the Cerne giant and now regarded as a Romano-British representation of Hercules. He had been to the British Museum and remarked: 'Figures of Hercules in the B.M. for comparison with the Cerne giant. The figures have always the club in the right hand; it is usually knotted. The left hand is usually turned out like the Cerne giant but it nearly always has the lion skin hanging on it. The private parts are always shown. Some have a serpent in the left hand.'

... 'Limpsfield Common. There are pits similar to those at Pen Pits on Limpsfield Common and also small pits or trenches within the mound, thrown up invariably to the west like those near Stroud.' Pen Pits were a controversial site in Somerset. Pitt-Rivers excavated there at his own expense and demonstrated that they were quarries. The report, which was privately printed, took the form of a report to the First Commissioner of Works: *Report on Excavations in the Pen Pits, near Pensel Wood, Somerset*, printed by permission of H.M. Commissioners of Works (London, 1884). It is an interesting case illustrating as it does his confidence in settling a matter of this kind with the spade, and also in that it was an official document published privately. There is a hint, as I have said above, that there was an element of this in the Cranborne Chase volumes of which the first appeared three years later.

Finally there is the negative interest of the books—what was left out. There are drawings of medieval buildings but clearly Gothic architecture was a very minor interest. The most striking feature is the complete lack of interest in natural history or geology. Fossils, plants or animals are barely referred to. Had the notebooks belonged to Lubbock for instance, whose book on *Ants, Bees and Wasps* had become a household word, we would have expected many drawings of insects and probably plants. The interests of Pitt-Rivers were closely confined to material culture.

When Pitt-Rivers gave up his salary (£250 p.a.—say the equivalent of £2,000 or £2,500 in 1975) in 1890 and became entirely an honorary Inspector his work did not cease. He continued to have matters referred to him by the Office of Works and to receive quite a large correspondence from the public on questions of preservation. He literally carried the title to his grave since he was still honorary Inspector at the time of his death. This perhaps is an indication of the importance that he attached to the office.

In trying to assess the importance of the Inspectorship of Pitt-Rivers we have to think ourselves back into nineteenth-century England. Before the creation of the welfare state in the early years of the present century (from which the basic modern Act of 1913 flowed) the degree of interference that was required for effective legislation was not attainable against the strength of property rights in Victorian England. This was official recognition of the state's obligation and 43 monuments formally passed into the care of the Commissioners of Works. Had the Act had greater powers the duties of the Inspector would have been correspondingly greater and this could have made serious inroads into the time spent on the excavations in Cranborne Chase. In many ways it was an ideal situation; he had the title without too heavy a burden of duties.

Pitt-Rivers was fairly complacent about the results of his activities, for he remarked in 1888: '... from my own observations, that there is very little damage to prehistoric monuments going on at the present time ...'. When one compares this with what he was saying around 1870 there must be some astonishment. Single-handed he could hardly have brought such destruction to a halt. The fact is of course that the assessment of the rate of destruction is highly subjective: it depends upon which end of the telescope you look down. A certain type of temperament (and Kate Stanley's description of his quarrels with his wife suggest Pitt-Rivers had this kind of temperament) develops from one or two cases of damage an anxiety (that can become an hysteria) that total destruction is imminent. It is a sort of apocalyptic vision with which we are only too familiar today. I suspect that conditions in 1870 had not been very different from what they were in 1888.

Nevertheless we must give credit where it is due. For over 30 years protection occupied the mind of Pitt-Rivers. It derived partly from a much greater knowledge than others of the value of prehistoric monuments and of the information that could be obtained from them. Lubbock had been responsible for the legislation but he acted with the knowledge that there was a man at his elbow who had the determination and strength of purpose to bell the cat. What was achieved was a partnership and I would not rate the contribution of Pitt-Rivers lower than Lubbock's, indeed in the long term it was very much greater. The imponderable but very real factor was the extent to which the title and office, influenced by the example of Viollet-le-Duc, provided the motivation for some monumental achievement, in this case the excavations and their massive publication in the Cranborne Chase volumes.

CRANBORNE CHASE I

'It being my will and intention that my own estates and the estates of the late Lord Bingley shall never vest in or belong to the same person so long as there shall be two sons of my said sister Marcia Fox or any issue male of such two sons in esse at the same time. . . .'[1]

Fox was the surviving son of the second son of Marcia and so was to benefit from this pregnant phrase in the will of George, 2nd Baron Rivers, made in 1823. It was however an astonishing piece of good fortune since Louisa, the elder sister of Marcia, had a son and grandson who had no less than 12 children. Most of these died in infancy and the eldest in 1867. The property then reverted to his uncle Horace who died in 1880, leaving no heir. It was as if the gods had willed that this large fortune should be placed at the disposal of the subject of our essay.

The will also stipulated that:

. . . within the space of one year next after he or they shall respectively become entitled as aforesaid take upon him or them respectively and use in all deeds, letters, accounts, and other writings. . . . shall sign and upon all other occasions whatsoever the surname of Pitt-Rivers either alone or in addition to his or their surname. And also shall take and use the arms of my family of Pitt either alone or in addition to any other arms. . . .[2]

The London Gazette of 4 June 1880 announced the Royal licence authorizing Fox to

take and use the surnames of Pitt-Rivers in addition to and after that of Fox and bear the arms of Pitt quartering in the first quarter with those of Fox, and that his issue may take and use the surname of Pitt in addition to and after that of Fox. . . .

Thus Fox became Pitt-Rivers and his children Fox-Pitt.

The estate, which lies to the south-west of Salisbury on the north side of the Salisbury–Blandford road, was estimated to extend over 24,942 acres in Dorset and 2,762 acres in Wiltshire. For Succession duty purposes the gross annual income on the estate was reckoned to be £27,477 4s 6d and the net annual income £22,897 13s.[3] At his death for estate duty purposes the aggregate gross value of the property was £414,586 7s 6d and of personal property £112,226 7s 6d. These figures give some indication of the complete transformation in the fortunes of Fox at the same time as he changed his name to Pitt-Rivers.

The area of the Chase was an unusual one. Although it contains native settlements of the Roman period there are no villas or towns, which suggested to the mind of the late R. G. Collingwood that this kind of country was an Imperial estate owned by the Emperor and run by his officials.[4] In the Middle Ages the area formed part of the honour of Gloucester, but had been in the hands of King John for a number of years due to his marriage to Isabel, daughter and co-heiress of William, Earl of Gloucester. He paid 14 visits to Cranborne and from the expenditure recorded in the Pipe Roll in 1207–8 it is reasonably inferred that he built the thirteenth-century house that forms the core of the Manor House at Cranborne.[5] The association here is authentic but was probably transferred thence to King John's House, Tollard Royal, owned by Pitt-Rivers, where the manor house which bears that name has no recorded association with King John and belongs indeed to the reign of his successor. In the late seventeenth century the Chase became separated from the manor of Cranborne, and so the former had constituted a separate estate from then until Pitt-Rivers inherited it.

Cranborne Chase is used in two senses, first the full outer Chase extending from Salisbury to Blandford and Shaftesbury to Wimborne, and second in the restricted sense covering an area about 10 miles long and 3–4 miles wide to the west of Cranborne. In 1828 it contained about 2,000 deer. It had been maintained by a Steward, with his Foresters and Woodwards, but by the nineteenth century the lodges had been appropriated for keepers. Rushmore Lodge where Pitt-Rivers lived was on the site of one of these lodges reconstructed by Lord Rivers as a mansion in c. 1760. The long wooded drive up to the mansion, now used as a school, still gives one a feeling of the Chase. The temple of Vesta that is seen on approaching the school was erected by Pitt-Rivers in 1890, at a cost of £1,792, to commemorate the birth of his eldest son's first son, George Henry Pitt-Rivers (10). Not being a manorial seat there is no village or church. The nearest village is at Tollard Royal with medieval hall and adjoining parish church in which the wife of Pitt-Rivers and his children are buried.

It must be remembered that Pitt-Rivers had neither been accustomed to, nor living in expectation of great wealth: how would such a serious-minded man react to riches of this kind? We are fortunate in that he kept a detailed account of his personal expenditure that survives in two large volumes recently deposited at the Dorset County Record Office, Dorchester,[6] which throw a good deal of light on this matter.

The accounts run from 1881 to 1901, being maintained for a short while after his death. In the first four years he tried to distinguish estate from personal expenditure, but gave this up in 1885. From then on he

10 The Temple of Vesta (built 1890) at Rushmore Lodge

simply dealt with disposable income, although it is clear that some items (like the costs of the Museum) must have been met from an estate account. If we take the expenditure, receipts and balance in round figures over a period of ten years, 1885–1894, it gives a fair idea of his resources. These figures are in pounds of the late nineteenth century, so very much larger sums in modern values are involved:

	Receipts	Expenditure	Balance
1885	£19,553	£17,659	£1,894
1886	£18,668	£13,953	£4,714
1887	£18,679	£14,762	£3,918
1888	£20,023	£15,022	£5,900
1889	£18,965	£16,070	£2,895
1890	£20,092	£17,597	£2,495
1891	£19,558	£15,550	£4,008
1892	£17,347	£15,569	£1,779
1893	£16,571	£16,335	£216
1894	£19,339	£15,225	£4,114

Pitt-Rivers is sometimes portrayed as a reckless spend-thrift but the accounts certainly do not bear this out. Indeed the mere fact that he kept accounts would suggest that this was not the case. Once we examine them and find that almost invariably his receipts exceeded his outlay then it is even more apparent that he kept a close hold on expenditure. If therefore he made a major purchase he had a clear knowledge of how this would affect his annual budget. A fortune of this size allowed a fair latitude but he was certainly not reckless, or at least not after the first year or two.

For the first four years the expenditure is put under 26 headings and from 1885 onwards there is an itemised list under each heading.[7] The 26 headings varied slightly in the course of the years, so that for example XIX, *Scientific Expenses* was later XVII or XX. Nevertheless the list of headings in 1881 gives a fair idea of what it remained throughout. It was as follows:

      I   *Home and household expenses*
     II   *Furniture and Art Objects Bought*
    III   *Stables*
    IV   *Woods and Gardens*
     V   *Bailiff and Farm*
    VI   *Sporting Expenses including keepers etc.*
   VII   *Rates, taxes and insurance*
  VIII   *Building expenses*
    IX   *Road making*
     X   *Journeys*
    XI   *Children*
   XII   *Clothes*
  XIII   *Doctor's expenses*
  XIV   *Rents paid*
   XV   *Repairs*
  XVI   *Transport*
 XVII   *Books and maps*
XVIII   *Succession duty*
  XIX   *Scientific Expenses including subscriptions to Societies,*
          purchase of objects, Excavations and Explorations.
   XX   *Mr Creech's (the agent) account*
  XXI   *Subscriptions, charities and presents*
 XXII   *Law expenses*
XXIII   *Land and homes purchased out of yearly income*
XXIV   *Miscellaneous*
 XXV   *Carpentery Establishment*
XXVI   *Jointures, annuities, pensions,*
          interest on mortgages

This was a period of high spending for English landed society and no doubt most of the headings would have appeared normal in any similar household of the period. There is heavy spending on the furniture and art section throughout the period, especially on pictures for both Rushmore and Tollard Royal. Books and maps in section XVII and of course scientific expenses reveal his particular interests. The latter, which covers the costs of excavations, will be discussed in the next chapter. Two new headings that appear from 1893 are *Menagerie and Fancy Stock* and *Sports and Pastimes*. The first referred to the yaks, reindeer and other animals that the General tried to breed and the latter mainly to increased outlay at the Larmer Grounds.

Some space must now be devoted to what was in many ways the most curious aspect of the 20-year Cranborne Chase episode. This was the attempt by Pitt-Rivers to woo the public, to persuade them to come to the rather remote part of the Wiltshire/Dorset area where he lived. The record of this is best preserved in the now rarely obtainable *A short Guide to the Larmer Grounds, Rushmore; King John's House; the Museum at Farnham; and Neighbourhood* (privately printed, editions of 1894 and 1900). It is important to remember that the motivation was entirely different from a modern safari park or fun-fair attached to a large house, where the purpose is commercial, to make money. Pitt-Rivers carried the full cost himself; all the visitor did to enter at any one of these three places, the Larmer Grounds, King John's House or the Museum was to sign his name in a book. What then was their purpose?

According to the late St George Gray the Larmer grounds were merely a means by which Pitt-Rivers allowed the general public to share in his good fortune. For a man who had not been accustomed to great wealth, who had come as an intruder from outside to replace an earlier family in its seat, such conduct was understandable and Gray may be partly right. In 1891 Pitt-Rivers himself explained the matter in terms which at once relates it to his earlier life[8] and indeed shows that it was—one might say—a fairly coherent strategy.

I hold that the great desideratum of our day is an educational museum in which the visitors may instruct themselves. . . . The knowledge of the facts of evolution, and of the processes of gradual development, is the one great knowledge that we have to inculcate, and this knowledge can be taught by museums, provided they are arranged in such a manner that those who run may read. The working classes have but little time.

Typology forms a tree of progress and distinguishes the leading shoots from the inner branches. . . .

It is to the larger and smaller tradesmen that such things as museums appeal but they must be supplemented by other inducements to make them attractive. Within a short distance of the museum I have formed a recreation ground, called the Larmer grounds. . . .

Bicycling is an institution that must not be overlooked in any project for the improvement of the masses.

Nowadays because of the motor car, it is fairly easy to persuade the public to come in large numbers to the remotest country house. It was quite a different matter to go to the nearest station by train and then hire a horse-drawn vehicle or walk, even if the bicycle was just beginning to make people more mobile. Nevertheless, in spite of this the annual attendance figures, published in 1900, show how successful he was: 15,351 (1887) and 44,417 (1899) at the Larmer Grounds, 5,706 (1888) and 12,611 (1899) at the Museum and 4,346 (1891) and 12,800 (1899) at King John's House.

The three institutions referred to are quite long distances apart if one is on foot. It will be useful now to deal with each in turn, starting with the Larmer grounds, the earliest to be formed and also the part surviving best to the present day.

It is possible that Pitt-Rivers had decided to create the Larmer pleasure grounds before he inherited the property, since he seems to have chosen this wooded site and erected the round temple in 1880. The choice as we have said (p. 12) was probably prompted by childhood recollections of the Black Fen pleasure grounds at Bramham Park. What indeed more natural than that a man of a cadet branch of the family who suddenly found himself in possession of a large fortune should imitate the ancestral home. The timber-framed caretaker's cottage was added in 1881, Boehm's bronze statue of *The hunter of early days* in 1883 and the bandstand in 1886. It is probably fair to say that it started off as as a park occasionally open to the public, but in 1885 became pleasure grounds normally open to the public.

The Larmer tree was where King John was said to have met his huntsmen (*see* p. 76). The Caretaker and Keeper wore costumes recalling those of the former Chase keepers. The public were invited to picnic in the grounds and cutlery and crockery were provided; liquor had to be brought. There were eight quarters each provided with arbour, seats and table, which have whimsical names: Owls, Cats, Yaks, Stags, Hogs, Hounds, the Vista and Band View. Pitt-Rivers had formed a private band of estate workmen who wore a special uniform and played on Sundays in the grounds; after its disbandment performances were given by a local militia band. German skittles, bowls and swings were provided in the shrubbery. Sunday was the main day at the Larmer Grounds, and this caused some controversy with strict observers of the Sabbath.

The accounts record the expenses of firework displays, of hiring singers and entertainers and so on. During the last five years of his life Pitt-Rivers made some remarkable additions to the Larmer grounds: the singing stand (1895), the dining hall (1896), the Japanese bronze pony (1897), the Oriental Room (1895), the Upper Indian House (1898) and the India Room (1899). The Oriental room contained a Moulton-ware chimney piece from the Viceroy's Reception Hall at Lahore. The Indian houses were bought from an Exhibition at Earls Court or were imitations made to represent them.

It will be noticed that the oriental additions were made about the time of the Diamond Jubilee in 1897. This was the Indian period of the Queen when the Durbar Room was added to Osborne House in the Isle of Wight. The buildings in the Larmer grounds, which served as summer houses, have been regarded as works of extreme eccentricity in

Pitt-Rivers, but I am not sure that the chief motive was not patriotism, engendering the same sort of exuberance that prompted many towns to erect clocks in honour of the Queen. The revelry in the Larmer grounds resembled and indeed was entered into in much the same spirit as the revelry on the pier of a Victorian seaside resort. Behind it all stood the serious-minded figure of the General, who gave away the prizes at the sports and acted as a remote headmaster figure.

Apart from the Larmer grounds there was the 'fancy stock' (reindeer, llamas, zebus, kangaroos, yaks, etc.) maintained at Rushmore and which provided an added attraction. A small hotel was also built near the museum. In addition he created a golf links. These were the sugar on the pill so to speak for behind the fun lurked serious education in the form of the two museums. Even if only a few who came for pleasure drank from the fountain of knowledge much good had been done. The whole concept was decidedly Victorian.

The idea of a private museum as a method of education was a familiar one in Victorian England. The Queen and the Prince Consort had erected a timber building beside the Swiss cottage at Osborne where the royal children could form their own collection into a museum in order to instruct themselves. There was, then, nothing odd in the decision of Pitt-Rivers to create a museum nor that, as it was situated miles from any town and railway station, it should consist of a collection of agricultural implements and peasant handicrafts.[9]

He directed himself at first to the agricultural workers, but it was difficult to kindle interest in the Victorian farm labourer: 'Hodge, though better off than he has ever been before, is in a lower condition, morally and mentally, than at any previous period.'[10] It was necessary therefore for the blandishments to be re-orientated towards the more urbanised lower middle classes. 'Architectural features, handsome halls and corridors are impediments . . .'[11] The purpose of the museum was to allow the nature of cultural evolution through 'typology' to be grasped, and hence the distractions of an elaborate building were to be avoided. For this reason no doubt Pitt-Rivers did not erect a new building for his museum but adapted an old one.

He chose a two-storeyed mid-nineteenth-century brick building[12] which had once been used as a school for gypsies but later reverted to its original use as a farmhouse. At each end flanking wings were added to match the original, and from the north wing a brick gallery was extended backwards and turned through a right angle. The 1894 guide shows this plan with a L-shaped gallery hidden behind the façade of the building. As the collections grew, however, another gallery had to be added to the north to give a T-shape and finally another extension to the south. As the latter projected beyond the façade it was built in mock timber-framing. The northern gallery was built like the others with brick buttresses and lit by roof-lights. Roof-lighting was much favoured in

11 A contemporary photograph of the Rushmore Band

this period and had considerable security advantages for a museum.

The earlier collection of Pitt-Rivers had been kept at his home until 1874 when it had gone to Bethnal Green. It had been finally transferred to Oxford University in 1884. He had kept back a small part, consisting of peasant carvings, for the new museum but the greater part of the collections for this were formed by purchase in the period he was at Cranborne Chase. As we have seen, both his personal accounts and the Inspector's notebooks show that he was ceaselessly purchasing material of the most varied kind.

On entering the building (**14**) through the south wing, rooms 1–3 contained peasant costume, carvings and utensils. Room 4 in the north wing contained ancient and medieval pottery on one side, modern pottery in the middle and locks and keys on the other side. This had been a subject that had interested Pitt-Rivers from at least the time of his excavations at Caesar's Camp, Folkestone. The only book of which he was author that was published by a commercial firm, not printed privately, *On the Development and Distribution of Primitive Locks and Keys*, had appeared in 1883. The book, which is excessively rare today, was his only monograph on an aspect of material culture and illustrates how he still retained his earlier interest during the Cranborne Chase period. As so often the point that impresses one is how he started from first principles, and really owed nothing to any predecessor. He was indeed laying down how the subject should be developed.

Rooms 5 and 6, the north wing and gallery contained a wide range of antiquities (ancient British, Silesian, Etruscan, Swiss, Oriental etc.) in the wall-cases, while on the tables ranged down the middle were models of the excavated sites of Woodcuts (room 5) and Rotherley (room 6). Models were indeed a great feature of the museum, which contained well over 100 of them. They were not model reconstructions ('models' in the modern jargon), but solid models in wood (mahogany) or hollow ones consisting of a wire frame covered with plaster of Paris. They were created from a closely contoured plan of the site, hence the great

12 A performance in progress at the singing stand of
Larmer Grounds: contemporary photograph.

13 The Indian House, Larmer Grounds

emphasis on contours in the Cranborne Chase volumes. It was not merely a method of record but a necessity for model-making. These panoramic models of earthworks, partly excavated, will recall cadet force panoramas to some readers, and no doubt their pedigree is a military one extending back to fortification models at Sandhurst and the United Services Institution.

Room 7 extending southwards contained more models of tumuli, collections to illustrate the history of enamelling and models of crosses. Most early Christian crosses stand in the open and inevitably deteriorate with the weather; it was the intention of Pitt-Rivers to make models as a permanent record of the decoration they bore before it was lost.[12a] The south-eastern 'timber-framed' gallery was evidently built to house the agricultural implements, which as we have seen were one of the main raisons d'être for the museum. The north gallery contained much more miscellaneous collections to illustrate the history of glassmaking, embroideries, lamps etc. The residence for the custodian was behind the main block while on the south-western part of the site was a nordic horse-mill brought from the Isle of Lewis.

The heterogeneous nature of the collection was made even more manifest by the arrival of the Benin bronzes at the end of the century. Benin had been taken by a punitive expedition on 17 February 1897, and the expedition was returning to England by 22 February. The accounts show that Pitt-Rivers was already buying up groups of bronzes in 1897 and the catalogue of his collection, *Antique Works of Art from Benin* (1900) appeared at about the time of his death. It was a very rapid piece of work. Posterity has approved the judgement of Pitt-Rivers, and indeed the enormous market value of the bronze figures in post-war years caused them to be among the first objects to be dispersed before the final break-up of the collections.

These lacked coherence and the average visitor was probably bewildered by the densely packed exhibits. The normal person is usually not impressed by typology and is indeed sceptical of its significance except for museum display. At least the Oxford collection was coherent, however bewildering its arrangement was to the visitor, but at Farnham there was a series of collections representing the different interests of the owner. You might visit it to see one or other of his particular activities that interested you but hardly for broad instruction. In the modern jargon the General was not a communicator; he had an aristocratic disdain for popularisation. This is what endears him to the scholar.

It remains now to deal with King John's House, Tollard Royal. The name is applied to a building later than John's reign and, as we have seen, is a transference from the Manor House at Cranborne. The house lies to the south-east of the parish Church,[13] and consists basically of a first-floor hall oriented east/west, with traces of a contemporary latrine tower at the south-west end and a seventeenth-century cross range on the east end. Most of the thirteenth-century two-light windows were exposed and partly restored by Pitt-Rivers in 1889,[14] when he carried out much work on the structure and excavated the adjoining area.

The exhibition in the house was intended to illustrate the history of painting and pottery-making. This valuable collection, containing paintings by Giovanni Bellini, Tintoretto and others, was the fine arts section of the main collection housed at Farnham.

The papers recently presented to the Salisbury Museum have thrown light on other activities at Rushmore in the two final decades of the last century. Pitt-Rivers evidently had political ambitions since there is a draft of a speech as a Parliamentary candidate[15] and a great many papers from 1888–9 when he stood unsuccessfully for the County Council. Unlike Lubbock—and the unrequited aspirations of Pitt-

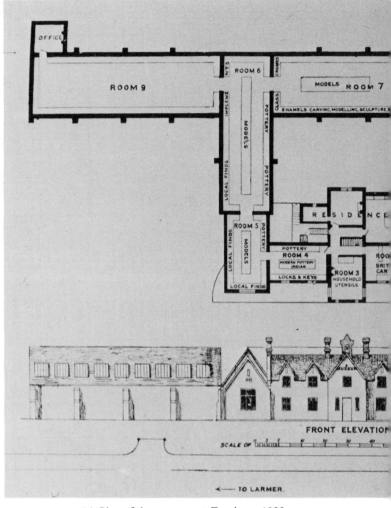

14 Plan of the museum at Farnham, 1900

Rivers give a certain piquancy to their relationship—who had considerable political gifts, Pitt-Rivers had no aptitude for politics. The speeches are of interest mainly for the light they throw on the speaker himself and particularly on the extent to which his ideas on evolution had penetrated his everyday thinking. They provided his opponents with material for accusing him of atheism. Here is an example, the abbreviated opening section of an address to the Handley Branch of the Primrose League in 1888:

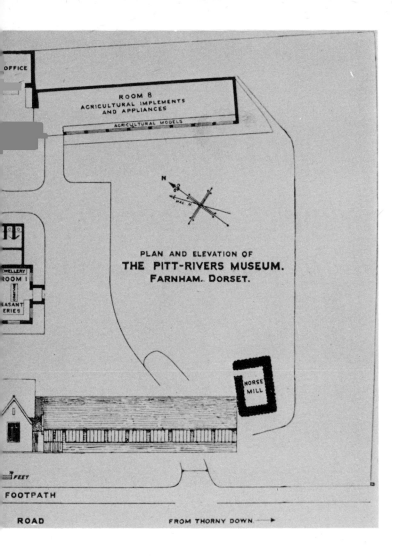

PLAN AND ELEVATION OF
THE PITT-RIVERS MUSEUM.
FARNHAM. DORSET.

Having been asked to take the Presidency of the Handley branch of the Primrose League I wish briefly to state my views for doing so. . . .

I confess that I am not enamoured of political life at the present time, it never was at a lower ebb than now. So long as party was subservient to political principle government went on well enough but of late principle on both sides has been made entirely subservient to party interests and I believe the country will be ruined if it goes on much longer.

As I am addressing conservatives I will speak of the shortcomings of conservatives in this respect. We all know what scoundrels our opponents are but we are not always impressed with the fact that we are great humbugs ourselves. The proper function of Conservatives is conservatism. How are we performing that function?

The progress of the world is regulated and properly so by antagonisms as Darwin, Huxley, Herbert Spencer and just recently Sir William Grove has impressed upon us. This is an age of science and we should listen to the voice of scientific men; they are our instructors. They see the affairs of the world from a higher standpoint than political men who are merely wire-pullers and self-interested partisans. The proper function of conservatism is to serve as a check upon violent changes.

Also among the papers at Salisbury are some 2,500 letters received by Pitt-Rivers from 1881–99, which is certainly not a complete series.[16] The most interesting group of correspondents socially were perhaps the clergymen, some of them occupying livings of which Pitt-Rivers was patron. The part they played in rural society is worthy of more study than there is time for here. Perhaps the largest group consisted of professional colleagues, many of long years' standing, like Canon Greenwell who still adopted something of a master-and-pupil attitude. The most numerous letters in this class are from H. J. Moule, Curator of the newly founded Museum at Dorchester, who wrote at great length about pottery.

As we have seen, the death of Rolleston in 1881 had deprived Pitt-Rivers of one of his closest friends; the letters reveal that his place was taken by John Clavell Mansel-Pleydell. He is the author of 155 letters in the collection and sometimes seems to have been writing almost weekly. Although he had been trained as a lawyer his interests were scientific. He was a member of the Linnean and Geological Societies, founder member and President of the Dorset Natural History and Archaeological Field Club. He was an assiduous excavator as well as being the author of *Flora of Dorsetshire* (1874), *Birds of Dorsetshire* (1888) and *Mollusca of Dorsetshire* (1898). Pitt-Rivers prided himself on being a scientist—his excavations come under the heading of 'Scientific Expenses' in his personal accounts—and the main common ground in the case of both Rolleston and Mansel-Pleydell was 'science'. There were however many other points of common interest.

Mansel—he took the additional name Pleydell when he inherited his mother's property in 1872—had spent 30 years in the Militia, the Queen's Own Yeomanry Cavalry, and so had military interests. He was a substantial landowner with many more years of experience in estate management than Pitt-Rivers whom he occasionally advised. The filling of vacant livings in the gift of Pitt-Rivers was a matter of animated discussion. The matter which gave them the greatest satisfaction was political discussion. Mansel-Pleydell left the Liberal party on the issue of Home Rule, to which Pitt-Rivers was also opposed; many after-dinner hours must have been spent by the two men in political discussion. Mansel-Pleydell lived in the handsome eighteenth-century house of Whatcombe, south of Blandford, and the 'fraternisation' referred to in the letters apparently meant going over to Rushmore for dinner and talk, and returning the next day.

The collecting interests of Pitt-Rivers were well known and so he received a stream of letters from people offering to sell him objects. They might be dealers, people in straitened circumstances, explorers offering ethnological specimens and hoping to obtain money. The Larmer Grounds also generated much correspondence; requests to visit and letters of appreciation afterwards; letters from performers, letters from municipal authorities with intentions to form pleasure grounds of their own. The great Cranborne Chase volumes were privately printed and so could not be bought; consequently there were a stream of requests for these and letters of gratitude on receipt.

Pitt-Rivers's ninth and last child had been born in 1866. During the Cranborne Chase period the children all grew up and married except the youngest son, Arthur. Arthur was afflicted by that dread scourge of the Victorian world, consumption (tuberculosis), and the family had to watch helplessly as the fatal disease pursued its course. He died in 1895 and was buried in Tollard Royal churchyard with a Celtic cross of the type in which Pitt-Rivers was interested as head-stone. One recalls the early death of the father and elder brother of Pitt-Rivers.

The eldest son and heir, Alexander, was a weak character and a disappointment to his father. He was an artist and there seems to have been an artistic streak in many members of the family to judge by the 'drawing game' played at Rushmore.[17] In this game a drawing was made by a member of the family and then passed to another member who had to redraw it. The object was to see how much the final result differed from the original after it had passed through seven or eight hands. The second son, St George, who held advanced political views and stood for Parliament, quarrelled seriously with his father who partly disinherited him.

One has the impression of a man who was fairly isolated from his family; they never seem to have shown much interest in his activities. It is noteworthy that the annual accounts kept by Pitt-Rivers which were continued for a short while after his death in another hand (probably Alexander's) at once omitted the heading 'Scientific Expenses'. Not the least of the difficulties with which a man engaged in academic activities outside the academic ambience has to contend is an environment that can be unsympathetic and sometimes obstructive. There may indeed have been some hostility to the expenditure on excavation by the heirs if Bertrand Russell's story[18] is to be believed—of guests having to scramble for the rice-pudding, because so much money was spent on excavation that there was not enough money for food. It was told as a joke of course; the accounts quoted leave little doubt that there were ample resources to have enough rice pudding, and if a shortage did cause the guests to have to scramble for it then the true explanation was almost certainly to be found in the parsimony of Alice Pitt-Rivers. (*see* p. 18)

CRANBORNE CHASE II

'Having retired from active service on account of ill-health, and being incapable of strong physical exercise, I determined to devote the remaining portion of my life chiefly to an examination of the antiquities on my own property'.[1] In this clear statement Pitt-Rivers explained his reasons for undertaking his excavations. The reader of this volume will be able to add others: his earlier excavations in Sussex; the fact that his new estate had been a medieval hunting area and so the absence of agriculture had left the antiquities extremely well preserved; the appointment to Inspector which threw an aura of officialdom over his activities.

Of his ill-health there can be no doubt. The doctors' letters in the Salisbury collection[2] show that he suffered from diabetes and frequent testing of the sugar content of his urine was a part of his normal health routine. Against the permanent background of diabetes there were intermittent but sometimes very severe attacks of bronchitis. The ravages of ill-health are painfully obvious if the portrait of the tall handsome figure of the early 1880s is compared with the bearded, shrivelled old man of the photographs in the fourth and last volumes of the Cranborne Chase series. According to St George Gray he had grown his beard on doctor's orders to protect his throat, which we might dismiss had not the biographer of Lubbock told us that he had grown his beard on doctor's orders for the same reason.[3]

The starting point for any discussion of his excavations must be the section entitled 'Scientific Expenses' in the personal accounts.[4] These covered more than excavation: they contained some purchases not included in the Furniture and Art section and also in the early years subscriptions to learned societies. On the other hand some expenses reasonably arising from excavation were omitted: the board and lodging of the assistants, the costs of the models and so on. However, they clearly give a fair guide to the level of activity. They are as follows (to the nearest pound):

1881	£709	1885	£1,092	1889	£1,275
1882	£1,353	1886	£1,207	1890	£1,398
1883	£927	1887	£1,310	1891	£636
1884	£791	1888	£1,547	1892	£1,094

1893	£466	1896	£410	1898	£626
1894	£424	1897	£750	1899	£767
1895	£467				

Two or three points emerge from these figures. First, the most active period was 1885–90 which is what we might have expected, since it was during this period that the work forming the basis of the first three volumes of reports was carried out. Second, there is a very marked falling off in activity after that but something of a spurt in the last few years, due to publication of the fourth volume and the purchase and study of Benin bronzes, as well as excavation at Iwerne in 1897.

The background to the excavations of Pitt-Rivers is the state of English farming in the great depression of 1870–1914.[5] After a prosperous period in the middle of the century British agriculture was faced by falling prices for its products due to cheap imports. As Pitt-Rivers said: 'Against agricultural depression, caused by foreign competition it is impossible to contend.'[6] There was no apparent drop in his income over this period, although there had possibly been some reduction since the middle of the century. Tenant farmers were perhaps the worst hit although of course landlords were also affected. There was a substantial decline all over the country in the area under cultivation and it is estimated that the number of people employed in agriculture fell from one million to 700,000. There was therefore much less employment to be found on the land. Nevertheless the gains made by agricultural labourers in wages, from 11s. to 14s. a week held. In Dorset wages were low; the rise here had been 9s. to 12s. a week. In the 1890s Pitt-Rivers paid his labourers on excavation 15s. a week with beer money, which was then a generous agricultural labourer's wage.[7]

He employed 8–15 men on his earlier excavations but this later rose to 20 or even 25 at Iwerne, but rarely exceeded 30. A team of 15 men working for six months, October to April, at 15s. a week each would cost £292 10s. 25 men for 3 months would cost £225. These were the sort of labour-costs involved when work was at full pitch. The accounts show that he normally drew the money and paid the wages himself (15).

In 1888 Pitt-Rivers said: 'I shall resume the inquiry as soon as the harvest, if such it can be called this year, is over ...'.[8] Before mechanization the labour needs of farming varied enormously with the seasons of the year, so that during harvest a large labour-force was required and during the winter a minimal one. The General took advantage of this to take up the slack labour for excavation during the winter months. The early work in Cranborne Chase at Winklebury Camp, Woodcuts and Rotherley was all done in this way. Work started in September or October and continued until Christmas or sometimes up to March or April of the following year. This system broke down at Bokerly Dyke and Woodyates because of the health of Pitt-Rivers, so

15 The digging-team at South Lodge Camp

that work could be carried out only when he was well enough to be there. This might be at any time but was usually in the summer. In the later 1890s winter working was resumed, when an assistant was in charge and the General himself only made visits.

All the excavation in Cranborne Chase was done by agricultural labourers and there were no student assistants, nor indeed so far as we know volunteers, nor any of those male and female helpers that are so much in evidence on a modern excavation. It would have been impossible for Pitt-Rivers to have done the elaborate work he did without skilled help and so he created a small team of assistants. It is not quite clear when he started to recruit them since the earlier years of the accounts are not itemized, but James seems to have been at Winklebury in 1881. One assistant was a clerk to assist the Inspector in his duties. When the team emerges into the printed record in the first Cranborne Chase volume there was an assistant (James) and two sub-assistants (Reader and Tomkin) but it rose to 4 or 5 in the next few years and then fell back to two or to one. These assistants—who were the most unusual feature of the whole Cranborne Chase episode—were the essential element in the excavations and deserve closer attention. During the period the list of them is as follows:

NAME	DATES OF SERVICE	TITLE	REMUNERATION	SUBSEQUENT CAREER
F. James	?1881–91	Assistant	£150 p.a.*	Maidstone Museum
W. S. Tomkin	?1882–90	Sub. Asst.	£84 p.a.	Waterlow Bros Ltd.
G. W. Reader	1885–89	Sub. Asst.	? £72 p.a.	
C. W. Gray	1888–92	?	? £72	Canada
H. Gray	1888–99	Clerk (Secretary)	£24–65 p.a.	Oxford & Taunton
C. E. Flower	1890–94		£72 p.a.	
G. W. Johnson	1896–1900	Draughts-man	£72 p.a.	
H. S. Toms	?1890's	Sub-custodian clerk		Brighton Museum
Peacock	1895 (3 months)	Draughts-man	£72.	

* Possibly James did not live in since his salary was markedly larger than the others.

It is important to remember that the 'clerks' were normally young men, although the younger Gray was recruited as a boy and only paid £24 p.a. at first. They slept at the museum, were fed by the Rushmore housekeeper (at least in the 1890s), and were paid at a rate that was not much more than that of a higher servant or bank clerk.[9] H. St George Gray, for instance, after 10 years' service was only paid £5 12s. 6d. a month with board. On the other hand those who already had some experience or qualification like Tomkin, Flower or Johnson were paid as much as 30s. or £2 a week. The payments were made at irregular intervals of one, two or three months and the rate of payment is difficult to calculate because sometimes extra payment was due for expenses, or there may have been a period of holiday on half-pay. When they were away from Rushmore on excavation, as at Wansdyke, there was an extra payment of three pounds a month. It should be noted that compared with other clerks of the period they were well paid—taking into account the free board and lodging.

Assistants had different although overlapping functions. They were called clerks or assistants and according to Pitt-Rivers the first three were trained in surveying by himself. They were all expected to assist in surveying in the excavations. As many as five were employed but three was the optimum number: one directed the excavations in the absence of Pitt-Rivers, one was a draughtsman and illustrator and one acted as clerk or made models. The elder brother of H. St George Gray, C. W. Gray, made the models of the crosses; he did not apparently enjoy a happy relationship with Pitt-Rivers and emigrated to Canada (although he later returned and applied to Pitt-Rivers for a reference). The most interesting in many ways was Tomkin, who has left us those charming drawings of Pitt-Rivers acting as scale when he was on tours of inspection. He was evidently a skilled draughtsman and the accounts show that he was sent on courses at the Polytechnic in London in 1889 for photography and drawing. Perhaps this was where he made the contacts that secured him a job with a printing house soon after.

In 1889 a camera was purchased and about the same time a Remington typewriter. The first made the sort of sketching done by Tomkin superfluous, as he no doubt realized. The publication of the first two Cranborne Chase volumes and the increasing number of visitors to the Larmer grounds spread the fame of Pitt-Rivers far and wide, and this led to an increase of correspondence and burden of clerical duties. H. St George Gray who had been recruited in 1888 in his teens (he remained with the General until July, 1899) largely coped with this increasing burden of clerical work. Johnson still appears in the Accounts as Secretary of the Museum in 1901 after the death of the General.

The cost of the excavations in Cranborne Chase was extraordinarily low. For a period of a year it was possible to employ three assistants full-time and 15 labourers for six months for within £600. One of the main reasons for the cheapness of the work was the lowly status of the 'clerks'. They had no professional qualification and were paid a modest fixed wage; there was no career structure and no question of increments. In the paternalistic household in which he found himself the assistant could not marry without financial loss. Furthermore he had no real qualification which would allow him to find a job outside. One clerk, Peacock, left after about three months. Three subsequently went into museums but others disappeared into other walks of life. The lowly status of the clerks made the excavations financially possible and allowed Pitt-Rivers to train the staff to the form he wanted. On the one hand it was a skilfully organized system which produced astonishingly impressive results for little outlay, but on the other it was hardly likely to throw up a successor.

The concluding section of this last chapter will be devoted to the excavations in Cranborne Chase, the climax of the book and in many respects of our subject's career. I hope that the reader will not feel this to be an anti-climax when he is told that it is not proposed to describe the excavations in detail. There are several reasons for this.

The format and style of this work does not lend itself to the reproduction of plans and figures with detailed text that this would require. Furthermore, the excavations themselves were almost essays in method which can only be fully savoured by dipping into the great quarto volumes themselves:

These volumes, containing the evidence upon which the results are based, are intended for workers only and it appears preferable to retain the privilege of presenting them privately, to those to whom they may perhaps be useful in conducting similar investigations.[10]

The Romano-British excavations, the descriptions of which fill the first three volumes, were very skilfully re-interpreted by Professor Christopher Hawkes[11] at the meeting of the Royal Archaeological Institute in Salisbury in 1947. His article is indispensable for understanding the original work although possibly the re-interpretation now needs re-interpretation yet again in order to take account of changing views since then.

It is perhaps best to treat the matter chronologically. Almost as soon as he had inherited the property in 1880 Pitt-Rivers had started excavating barrows near the house (while Rolleston was still alive). Early in 1881 he went on a holiday in Egypt where he discovered palaeolithic flints in the concreted gravels of the Nile terraces near Thebes, a matter which gave rise to some controversy at a later date. In the Autumn of 1881 he embarked on his first full winter season of excavation at Winkelbury Camp, an Iron-Age hill-fort on the estate. The work comprised the usual sections and excavation of neighbouring barrows, during the course of which an Anglo-Saxon cemetery came to light.[12]

Hitherto the excavations had not been very different from what he had already done in Sussex. There was something of a pause, then, for the next two years when he was no doubt pre-occupied with locks and keys and his new duties as Inspector, including the excavations at Pen Pits in Somerset. In the Autumn of 1884 he embarked on an excavation of an entirely new kind at the Romano-British site on Woodcuts Common just outside the park of Rushmore. This occupied him throughout the winter of 1884–85 and in the latter part of 1885 up to Christmas, and in the following winter of 1886–87 he turned his attention to the analogous site of Rotherley about a mile away.

What caused Pitt-Rivers to decide to transfer his attention from the familiar type of site, barrows or hill-forts, to a totally unfamiliar kind of objective is not at all clear. It may be that he felt he had exhausted the possibilities of the former. In view of his avowed predilection for prehistoric remains (p. 60) it was a bold decision. Roman coins bearing the names of Emperors, the dates of whose reigns are known, arrange themselves in a historical sequence—not in the evolutionary series which we had been told in the first season at Cissbury it was the purpose of the excavator to construct. He had come a long way.

It was a bold decision in another way. The surface indications in both cases consisted of low banks, humps and hollows covering several acres. In the case of Woodcuts there had been already a cursory excavation so there was some slight clue as to what to expect. How did you tackle such unpromising remains? All the experience that Pitt-Rivers had had from hill-forts was that the only permanent traces recoverable by excavation were disturbances in the natural chalk below the soil, and so he set about exposing the chalk surface:

... trenching the interior space, placing the men in line at working distance apart, digging down everywhere through the surface mould until the chalk beneath was reached and noticing carefully any irregularity in the latter. Where the mould went deeper it was dug out and in this way pits, hearths, ditches and irregularities of all kinds were cleared out and exposed.[13]

The results yielded by these methods are the celebrated plans of the Woodcuts and Rotherly.[14] They are plans of disturbances in the chalk, due only to human activities that penetrated the soil to reach the chalk. There were a few structures, notably the 'hypercausts' of Pitt-Rivers re-interpreted by Hawkes as corn-drying ovens. Essentially however there were two kinds of feature revealed: long snaking ditches, or 'drains' as they were called by Pitt-Rivers, and circular, sometimes bell-shaped, pits from one to several feet deep. The latter of course he had been familiar with from Mount Caburn days. It is unlikely that much drainage would be required on a permeable subsoil like chalk and the 'drains' of Pitt-Rivers are best interpreted as shallow ditches outside fences or hedges of somewhat irregular circular enclosures.

The principle of modern excavation is of course similar: to clear the surface of the chalk and locate disturbances. Greater interest however now attaches to the small disturbances, the post-holes or filled-in sockets in the chalk made to accommodate the base of timber uprights. If the pattern of post-holes can be determined a reasonable guess can be made as to the shape of the superstructure, or at all events the possible alternatives. Pitt-Rivers had uncovered post-holes at Mount Caburn but it is unlikely that his rather crude method of working with labourers exposed a clean enough chalk surface to show them. At all events he did not find them at Woodcuts although he did expose some at Rotherley.

The art of revealing patterns of post-holes was a technique that had been carried to a high level before the war in Germany, whence came the late Gerhard Bersu who excavated the Iron Age site of Little Woodbury, Wiltshire. This is a proper Iron Age site of say 500–200 BC, but Bersu's excavation showed it had consisted of a single large house; it was not a village. Pitt-Rivers had interpreted both Woodcuts and Rotherley as villages, where the individual house-sites could not be identified. On the basis of Little Woodbury Hawkes was able to re-interpret both as farmsteads, probably single round-houses also. Pitt-Rivers had regarded the pits as an enigma, confused by the fact that they had often been filled in and a human burial inserted in their upper part. On Bersu's interpretation they would have been storage pits for roasted grain, a view now generally accepted. If the Cranborne Chase area be regarded as part of an Imperial estate, then the people living there would have been expected to produce grain for the Emperor. The lower proportion of storage pits to assumed population at the two Cranborne Chase sites compared to Little Woodbury caused the fertile brain of Professor Hawkes to attribute this to the amount of grain that had to be paid to the Imperial tax-collectors, and most ingenious calculations have been done on this basis.

If the way of life of the inhabitants at Woodcuts and Rotherley was still Iron Age in style, their tools and ornaments were by way of contrast decidedly Roman. No one who turns over the pages of the first two Cranborne Chase volumes can fail to be astonished by the contrast between the squalidness of the place of living of the people described and the sophistication of their possessions: coins, fibulae, styli, pottery etc. Both sites were occupied from just about the time of the Claudian conquest up to the end of the third, or in one case into the fourth, century A.D. One of the great achievements of Pitt-Rivers is to have etched on our minds the picture that must have been presented by most of the inhabitants of Britain in the Roman period—a barbarous people, no doubt Celtic in speech, with a veneer of Mediterranean civilisation. It is not something that one readily appreciates in a Roman villa or town.

This may be a convenient point to consider the publication of the Cranborne Chase excavations. Strictly speaking they were never published since the records appeared in volumes which were privately printed and could be acquired only by presentation. The Salisbury letters record that they were bound either in paper, in cloth or calf. The book on locks and keys had been produced by a commercial publisher but the report on the Pen Pits excavations addressed to the Commissioners of Works was privately printed and this seems to have prompted the idea of bringing out later works in the same way. The curious design on the bindings is based on a decorated plaque of Kimmeridge shale found at Rotherley.

The unifying factor running through the four great quarto volumes is the plates, which are numbered continuously right through. The text is, indeed, very largely a series of descriptions of plates strung together as if the work had really been conceived of as an album of plates. There is a hint of this in one item[15] of the Salisbury collection where the text figures in volume II had been kept together as if they had been sent in as an afterthought. Volume IV is rather different in that photographic illustrations were used which give an altogether more graphic picture of the work. It has to be remembered that the volumes were only part of the record, for the plans (a few originals survive at Salisbury) were sometimes coloured and so look quite different from the published version. Again the culmination of the record derived from the laboriously measured contouring* was the model, either of wood or wire and plaster, with the contours and details painted on. Copies of the volumes were placed in the Farnham Museum, and in order to savour the full record the visitor had to look at the plates in the volume, read the description and then go and study the model.

The Relic Tables, which as we have seen (p. 55) were first developed at Mount Caburn, were used throughout the volumes, set up in small print and sometimes in horizontal columns. They were evidently drawn up by an assistant and are probably more reliable where there are discrepancies with the text, as for example in the case for the dates of the excavations at Woodcuts.

The predominantly Roman sites that Pitt-Rivers was dealing with yielded a profusion of finds which are elaborately treated, often being illustrated at natural scale. These range over pottery, coins, fibulae and other metal objects. Quite trivial objects wear a dignified air in these pages. The General had been interested in physical anthropology for some years and in view of the importance attached to skulls in the nineteenth century the lavish illustration and treatment of the skeletal material was to be expected. He invented a craniometer—a metal frame for supporting a skull to allow various measurements to be taken—now one of the prized exhibits of the Salisbury Museum. There is perhaps no item more illustrative of the labour and care in the excavations than the specially made wooden boxes to contain the long bones (now at Salisbury). Fashions have now changed and we regard this detailed treatment of the pathetic Romano-British skeletons from the storage pits as laboured. Views can change, however, and it may be that much more significance will one day again be attached to skeletal material of this kind.

One kind of record where Pitt-Rivers was well ahead of his time was in the treatment of the bone fragments of domestic and wild animals that littered the sites. As the excavation was virtually complete over the whole settlement he was dealing with more than a mere sample. The treatment was incredibly detailed, involving not only measurement and illustration, but also the killing of modern animals in order to compare their measurements with the bones of the ancient animals. From this Pitt-Rivers was able to infer that the Romano-British horse was comparable to a modern pony in size and that the sheep of the period resembled a St Kilda sheep of today. Comparisons of the bones of the animals available to the inhabitants can of course throw light on many other matters. It is of interest that as late as 1953 the author of a book

---

* Study of the original plan shows that the levelling, usually for contouring at 6 in. intervals, was not based on a grid and was a good deal less laborious than might be at first supposed.

on Prehistoric Europe was using the results of Pitt-Rivers' iden-
tifications to show the change from a woodland environment in which
pigs throve during neolithic times to open pasture to which sheep are
better adapted in Iron Age times.[16]

As we have seen, at the time he was appointed Inspector in 1882 Pitt-
Rivers had visions of executing some great *magnum opus* like the
French Inspecteur-General, Viollet-le-Duc. In fact there could hardly
be a greater contrast between the Cranborne Chase volumes and those
of the *Dictionnaire de l'Architecture*. What then was the origin of the
style of the former? One recalls the *Reliquiae Aquitanicae* of Lartet and
Christy, published many years before. Christy, then a rich man when
Fox was poor, had of course been a mentor of Pitt-Rivers in his collecting days. Both in private and in public the General laid emphasis on the
scientific nature of his work and probably he had in mind some great
zoological or botanical album in which a specie is illustrated in each
plate accompanied by a description, but where the plates are the essential feature of the work.

It is time now to return to the work of excavation. Pitt-Rivers described
his decision to transfer his attention from the Romano-British villages,
where he had dug, to the great dykes that lay to the north of them, and
faced north, as a logical step to relate one type of monument to another.
His skull measurements at Woodcuts and Rotherley suggested that the
dykes marked an ethnic barrier.[17] Considering his inconclusive work on
the Devil's Dyke at Flamborough in 1879 we may suspect that he
would not have tackled this type of linear earthwork again had not
chance suddenly suggested that the results were likely to be very
different in this case. The bandmaster of the Rushmore Band, Albert
Lawes, while passing along the Salisbury/Blandford road, saw a farmer
digging soil for top-dressing in Bokerly Dyke. The farmer told him of his
discovery of Roman coins on the surface while doing this, information
that Lawes passed on to the General. It was at once apparent that
datable objects were going to be found there and accordingly an
excavation that was to extend in intermittent campaigns over two years
was begun.[18]

Bokerly Dyke is briefly glimpsed by the motorist driving to or from
Salisbury along the Blandford road. On the south side of the main road
it consists of a substantial bank and ditch (in 1974 heavily overgrown
with scrub) meeting the road at an acute angle and visible as a small and
overgrown earthwork leaving the road on the north side in a north-
westerly direction. It is a defensive work facing north that extends for
some four miles. After running for a few hundred yards almost parallel
to the main road the dyke swings south-eastwards and then pursues a
sinuous course eastwards for two to three miles. About quarter of a mile
from the main road there is a slight return on the south side as if the

dyke had originally terminated at this point. This curious feature, to which we shall return, was christened the 'epaulment' by the General, from the vocabulary of nineteenth-century military fortification.

On the north side of the main road and close to it the line of the dyke is intersected by the line of Ackling Dyke, the Roman road from Salisbury to Badbury Rings, robbed out at this point but visible as a substantial bank (*agger*) running straight for miles on either side, though making a slight bend to the south just behind the dyke; this curious point of intersection of two ancient features, the dyke and the Roman road with the modern road, was christened by the General 'Bokerly Junction', a name that has of course become famous in archaeology.

Pitt-Rivers began work on 22 May 1888 by opening a section, 30 ft wide, through the dyke and ditch at the point of the discovery.[19] Abundant Roman remains were found in the bank and ditch, the latter proving to have a double bottom. This fact was pregnant with interest although its significance was not immediately apparent. The wealth of Roman remains indicated the close proximity of a Romano-British settlement, of interest in itself but of course archaeologically of the first importance because it meant that there was likely to be firm dating evidence at whatever point in the neighbourhood one dug on the dyke.

The General cleared several acres of top soil, on the north side of the modern road on both sides of the Roman road. The characteristic 'drains' or ditches, familiar from Rotherley and Woodcuts, came to light although forming more rectilinear patterns than in the two earlier excavations. They lay mainly on the north side of the Roman road where the settlement had evidently lain. Probably what was revealed was only a fraction of the settlement, which was clearly quasi-urban unlike the two earlier sites, and its main centre lay to the south-west of Bokerly Junction. We are manifestly dealing with one of the stations that occur at 10 or 12-mile intervals along Roman roads. It cannot be identified with certainty but it might be *Vindogladia* of the Antonine Itinerary.

The Roman station was an interesting enough discovery but the main objective of the excavation had been Bokerly Dyke itself. The results were remarkable and can be briefly outlined without entering into the intricate details that Christopher Hawkes has so skilfully worked out. The dyke as we see it is a work of three stages of construction. The first dyke did not reach Bokerly Junction, for after running from an unknown starting point westwards it terminated at the epaulment. It protected an area of downland to the south for an uncertain purpose. The Roman settlement at Woodyates and the Roman road were almost certainly still in use at the time, for this section of dyke was probably constructed in the early fourth century A.D.

The second stage of construction implied a much more drastic interference with the settlement and road, since the dyke was extended westwards from the epaulment to cut through settlement and road at the junction. It followed the present line until just before the Roman road, where it took a more southerly course than the existing dyke. This was the explanation for the double bottom in the ditch; the later re-excavation of a second ditch had formed a new profile. The part of the ditch that cut the Roman road was subsequently filled in and furnished with a metalled surface evidently with the object of bringing the road back into use. In the third and final stage the dyke was re-dug on a new more northerly line than the earlier course from the junction and the Roman road finally severed.

Baldly stated, such was the result of the very laborious work over two years. Dating evidence in the form of coins and pottery was abundant. It is a matter of common sense that a structure must be later than the material it contains, but the problem that confronts the archaeologist is that the structure may be a few days or several centuries later than the objects within it.

The General interrupted his campaign at Bokerly dyke to make test sections in the Wansdyke, north of Devizes. This was more difficult since there was no convenient adjoining settlement from which stray objects had been incorporated into the bank. Nevertheless he was able to satisfy himself that it contained Roman material and so could not have been thrown up before late Roman times.

Hawkes worked out dates for the three stages of Bokerly dyke that would place them in the fourth century and he would even associate them with recorded disturbances of that period. In view of the dyke's respect for the Roman station in the first stage and re-construction of the Roman road in the second this seems reasonable. Lurking in the mind of Pitt-Rivers was the need to demonstrate ethnic differences by skull measurement, and he preferred to see the work as a defence of Britons against Saxons. The Saxon settlement in this area was late, sixth century, and Hawkes argued plausibly that the much more extensive defence of the Wansdyke may be more reasonably attributed to that purpose.

Although there are of course Iron Age dykes at Colchester and elsewhere, since the excavation of Pitt-Rivers at Bokerly junction attribution of linear earthworks to the Dark Ages is regarded as normal unless proven otherwise. Furthermore the only way of tackling the date of these intractable monuments is to identify an adjoining site of known date and determine which is earlier. It was avowedly using such principles that the late Sir Cyril Fox tackled the Cambridgeshire dykes, although he lacked the resources of Pitt-Rivers to open up on such a large scale.

Excavation seems to have come to a halt for the three years 1891–3, evidently due to deterioration in the General's health. He was taken seriously ill at Devizes during the Wansdyke excavations and his severe attack of bronchitis in the early part of 1892 was thought by many to be a last and fatal one (the Salisbury letters make this clear). He spent a period of recuperation in France in the later summer of that year and evidently felt fit enough to resume operations in the next Spring.

We have seen that the General's interests had been avowedly prehistoric in Sussex and in Cranborne Chase prior to 1884. The great excavations of 1884–90 were on Romano-British monuments, but in 1893 he returned to his earlier interests, although this may not have been entirely intentional. The object of study was the small square or diamond-shaped enclosures on the downland which turned out to be Bronze Age in date, but this was not of course known before he started. In pursuit of one of these he turned his attention to the adjoining barrows of which the largest was a long barrow, Wor barrow, excavated in 1893–94.

The excavations up to 1896 were recorded in the fourth and last volume of *Excavations in Cranborne Chase* published in 1898. Pitt-Rivers did in fact carry out another excavation at Iwerne between September and December, 1897 which was to have formed the basis of a fifth volume. This he did not live to complete, but fortunately the matter was taken in hand by Professors Hawkes and Piggott for the meeting of the Royal Archaeological Institute at Salisbury in 1947. With the aid of the late Mr H. St George Gray, who directed the work for the General, it was possible to build up quite an intelligible account of the excavation.[20] As this is much more closely related to the earlier excavations it will be convenient to mention it briefly first.

The interest of the site at Iwerne is that although in the earliest stages of occupation the inhabitants seemed to have been living under very similar conditions to those at Woodcuts and Rotherley, they passed through later stages reaching a higher standard of life. From being completely barbarian they achieved a fairly high degree of civilisation. The first stage showed traces of 'drains' and storage-pits of the familiar kind with no recognizable dwellings. In the second stage (third century A.D.) a trench marking the robbed footings delineated a building measuring some 110 by 40 ft. Its width suggests that the span was too great for roofing without internal supports and that it was aisled. In the third phase (fourth century) a level platform had been excavated out of the slope and a long building, 25 ft wide with walls 3 ft 6 in. thick, had been created on it. We are in fact dealing with something like a normal Roman villa with a development comparable to that known elsewhere.

The quadrangular enclosures that Pitt-Rivers excavated in 1893–6 need be mentioned only briefly. There were three distinct examples—South Lodge Camp, Handley Hill Entrenchment and Martin Down Camp. The procedure used was that employed at Woodcuts

16 Excavation in progress at South Lodge Camp

or Rotherley; the chalk was bared all over the site and the ditches cleared out all the way round. The characteristic pits and drains of the other sites were absent and there were indeed no disturbances in the subsoil that might have provided some clue as to the activities that went on within the enclosures. Prehistoric structures rarely yield a prolific number of small objects, and the main advantage of the total excavation carried out by the General was that this obviously greatly increased the chances of finding datable material. The banks of these earthworks were low, so the most reliable dating evidence came from the ditches and in the case of South Lodge (16) and Martin Down earthworks the evidence was conclusive for a Bronze Age date. In the case of the Handley Hill entrenchment Pitt-Rivers felt doubts about the dating since a Roman coin occurred low down in the bank, and Professor Piggott, who examined the pottery from the ditch, is satisfied that the position in which a medieval jug occurred can leave no doubt that the earthwork itself belonged to the Middle Ages.[21]

Two rolled plans at Salisbury[22] show us how the work was carried out. Both are in pencil. In one case, where survey of a barrow was started and abandoned, rectangles with intersecting diagonals show setting out for preliminary contouring which was the initial operation. The working plan of South Lodge Camp shows a contoured plan at 6 ft to 1 in. in use, finds with depths being recorded in the margins all the way round. There was a colour key for finds of different periods. Such a method would hardly have been feasible on a Romano-British site where finds are very numerous, but was practicable on a prehistoric site where finds are scarce.

This survey of the Cranborne Chase excavations can be fittingly concluded by reference to the Wor Barrow excavation in 1893–4. Long barrows were a type of monument of which there had been extensive exploration before the days of Pitt-Rivers, notably by John Thurnam. The latter like the General was particularly interested in skulls and he it was who had enunciated the famous principle 'long barrows—long skulls; round barrows—round skulls.' The plate in volume IV[23] showing Wor Barrow with the ditch excavated and the mound intact, and a photograph with the mound excavated except for a column of soil left standing, is one of the most evocative of the methods of work of Pitt-Rivers and their difference from those of his predecessors. (17–20)

Wor Barrow was excavated in two campaigns in 1893 and 1894. In the first campaign the entire infilling of the discontinuous ditch was removed, a considerable undertaking when one bears in mind the dimensions of a Neolithic ditch of this kind. The finds in the filling were of a standard kind, antler picks and pottery, and as there was no pottery with the primary burials the dating evidence from the ditch was of crucial importance. The primary burial consisted of a small group of six skeletons at one end of the mound. The most interesting discovery,

17 Tackling the mound at Wor Barrow (contemporary photograph)

however, was that the mound covered a long rectangular pattern of slots in the chalk intended to hold continuous uprights for an enclosure or building, and it was evident that the corpses had originally been placed within this. Obviously this kind of communal burial practice was analogous to that employed in contemporary chambered tombs with their chambers constructed of stones. The point was recognized by the General and has been repeated many times since, although the opportunity to repeat the experiment of removing the whole mound of a long barrow has only rarely been possible, since resources of this scale have been available to excavators only on few occasions.

After the excavation of Wor Barrow the empty ditches were left open, and three years later Pitt-Rivers returned and re-excavated the filling that had accumulated in the intervening time.[24] The object of course was to determine how the filling had formed originally when the barrow was made. At first the chalk breaks away from the ditch sides to accumulate as rubble at the bottom. As this happens rapidly turf protects the lower part of the ditch sides but the upper parts will suffer from erosion for a long period, the lip of the ditch working its way further back as this proceeds. The excavated ditch will have a flared profile although the original sides must have been, if not vertical, certainly much steeper. Similar experiments have been carried out since, but have not added materially to the General's observations. In order to interpret the relative time that has elapsed since such deposits were

18 Wor Barrow: the mound removed

formed in the ditches the nature of the process of deposition must be understood.

This chapter cannot be concluded without reference to some of the precepts of Pitt-Rivers enumerated in the opening pages of the Cranborne Chase volumes, which have become the lore of the subject and profoundly influenced field-workers ever since. They do not constitute a considered philosophy but indicate an attitude that is entirely different from barrow-diggers of the eighteenth and nineteenth centuries.

Tedious as it may appear to some, to dwell on the discovery of odds and ends, that have no doubt, been thrown away by their owners as rubbish, and to refer to drawings, often repeated, of the same kind of common objects, yet it is by the study of such trivial details, that Archaeology is mainly dependent for determining the dates of earthworks; because the chance of finding objects of rarity in the body of rampart is very remote. The value of relics, viewed as evidence, may on this account be said to be in an inverse ratio to their intrinsic value.[25]

The paradox of the last sentence does not logically flow from the previous one and taken literally would be perverse and absurd. In the section at Bokerly Dyke the Roman coins obviously had an intrinsic value higher than the sherds of coarse pottery, but no one would doubt that equally their value as dating evidence was much higher. With some exaggeration, what Pitt-Rivers was saying was that the purpose of the excavator was to date the earthwork, and as the only tools for doing this

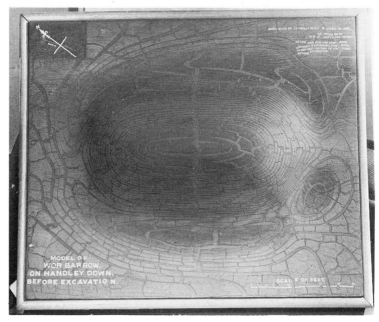

19 A model at Salisbury museum of Wor Barrow before excavation

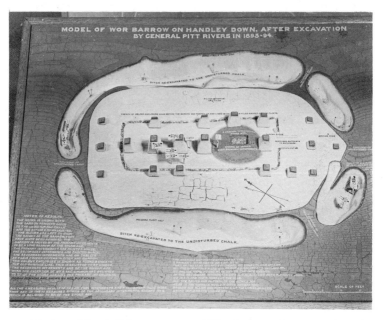

20 A model at Salisbury museum of Wor Barrow after excavation

were the 'odds and ends' they had to be made the subject of intensive study to extract the maximum chronological value: the objective of an excavation is not the collection of rare and valuable objects.

Yet the everyday life of the people is, beyond all comparison, of more interest than their mortuary customs. The desire to enrich our Museums is no doubt a great impulse to research, but even from that point of view, a carefully-made model, to scale, of any earthwork or building, in which a discovery has been made, is a much more interesting object in a collection, than the now familiar series of stone and bronze axes, spears, swords and urns, with which nearly all our Museums are supplied in such abundance, and with such unvarying uniformity, that they almost pall upon the visitor in search of something new.[26]

Canon Greenwell had indeed maintained that the object of excavation was to study the life of the people, but with the exception of Grime's Graves he had confined his attention to barrows. What astonishes us about Pitt-Rivers was his confidence in his ability to obtain useful information by digging as when he launched out on the excavation of Woodcuts for instance. This leads us to the next point. The volumes

... are not intended for casual readers. The record of an excavation takes about five times as long as the actual digging.[27] ... Much of what is recorded may never prove of further use, but even in the case of such matter, superfluous precision may be regarded as a fault on the right side where the arrangement is such as to facilitate reference and enable a selection to be made.[28]

It is in the reporting of archaeological excavations that the influence of Pitt-Rivers has been most permanent. The long and detailed report that takes five times as long to write as the excavation did to do; this is the normal procedure for the excavator. The specialist reports and detailed descriptions of the small objects and pottery: the form these take today stems in great part from the work of Pitt-Rivers.

Forty-seven years after the General's death Professor Hawkes re-interpreted a good part of his excavations, and it is very interesting to see whether the record was thorough enough to allow this. It is clear that the finds record was very thorough and so Hawkes was able to make detailed chronological alterations, especially at Woodyates. With regard to structures these could be re-interpreted, such as corn-drying kilns for hypocausts, but what had not been observed in the original excavation could not of course be re-interpreted. Woodcuts and Rotherley are unintelligible without some clue as to the house-plans which could only have been identified if post-holes had been recognized. The General was only dimly aware of the existence of post-holes and not at all of their use for identifying houses. This was not of course his fault, but nevertheless it does illustrate the fallacy of believing that your record can be so detailed that posterity can re-interpret it as it wishes. The chances are that posterity will be interested in something of which you have no knowledge and therefore never recorded. This point is worth making; nevertheless, the record made by Pitt-Rivers was so thorough that Hawkes could publish the unpublished work at Iwerne and re-interpret the other excavations.

A point that is often overlooked is the weight the General attached to scale of work: 'The most erroneous conclusions may be come to by confining the explorations to sections only and many of the most important objects may be missed.'[29] Total excavation was the desirable aim. It is really a question of resources. Fifteen labourers working 10 hours a day for a six or sometimes seven-day week could shift vast quantities of soil. One need only compare the huge swaths cut through Bokerly Dyke with the narrow trenches, hardly wide enough for a man to pass, cut through the Cambridgeshire dykes by the late Sir Cyril Fox, to see the point. In the past 20 years it has become feasible to emulate the scale of the General's work partly through mechanization and partly because the State has placed much greater resources at the disposal of archaeologists.

What Pitt-Rivers was saying clearly altered the whole nature of excavation. The objectives were quite different: it was not just a tedious removal of soil in order to reach the urn or Roman tessellated pavement but an end in itself. You set out not with the express purpose of making finds of great value, but with the intention of dating the earthwork from small, valueless finds in it, or of studying the life of the people in a settlement from the discarded bones of their domestic animals. Probably indeed you were not quite sure what information would be brought to light by the excavation but—and this is the important point—you were quite confident that significant additions to knowledge could be made in this way. From this—with all its virtues and faults—has arisen modern excavation, a costly operation with the uncovering of large areas, laborious recording and large reports. Praise or blame for this we must in large measure lay at the door of Pitt-Rivers.

CONCLUSION

Pitt-Rivers died at Rushmore on 4 May 1900 and was cremated at Woking soon afterwards. His wife and children were buried in Tollard Royal churchyard while he is commemorated by a carved urn at the west end of the church. In death as in life he is separated from his family, for in 1900 cremation was unusual, if not almost improper; it was the last act of defiance by a man who had a slight streak of the rebel in him. No one could have been so closely associated with T. H. Huxley in the 1860s without having some tinge of rebellion in him. Perhaps indeed there is a hint of the rebel in most archaeologists, particularly in prehistoric archaeologists who lay claim to a special knowledge of our hidden past. Be that as it may, the time has now come for a general review of the life of Pitt-Rivers as set out in the chapters of this book to see if threads can be drawn together that will allow some general conclusions to be drawn.

Of the childhood and boyhood of Fox we know too little to be able to make any serious observations. The early death of his father and his up-bringing by his Scottish mother were clearly highly formative matters for the young Fox, but we are too ill-informed about Lady Caroline Fox or life in St James's Square to know how they compared with the boy's infancy in Yorkshire. Of the circumstances that led to his withdrawal from Sandhurst or how he completed his education from July 1941 to May, 1845 we are unfortunately quite ignorant.

The young Fox really swims into our ken in the Alderley letters of the 1850s, although he is seen through hostile eyes and normally presented in a bad light. Indeed we know that the Editor of the letters suppressed some that were too indelicate. His courtship with Alice was a genuine love affair on both sides, and after coming to grief initially because of his lack of means the situation was retrieved by his brother's death making him sole heir. It is most unlikely that Alice played much part in the in-tellectual development of Fox but the stimulating ambience of the Stanley household and guests almost certainly sparked off an interest in matters of the mind.

Whether he began testing the new rifles at Woolwich in 1850 or 1851 is not clear, but by 1852, when he went to study training methods on the Continent, the aspect of the new arm that was to be his special interest was clearly to be training others in the use of it. His appointment as Captain Instructor at the new School of Musketry at Hythe (1853) and the appearance of the much altered *Instruction of Musketry* (1854) showed where his true interests lay. His 1858 lecture showed that he had an excellent grasp of the technical development of the rifle but mechanical invention was not his *forte*; judging distances, elaborate grading by ability and so on, the practical aspects of the rifle's use are what interested Pitt-Rivers. Inevitably one makes comparisons with Cranborne Chase in later life.

The short but grim experiences of the Crimea and the subsequent two years in Malta so far as we know had no great effect on his intellectual life. The attraction of the rifle was its general introduction into the army in 1853–5; and although of course very interesting changes—notably from muzzle to breach-loading—were to take place, its intellectual interest was limited, particularly when studied on the ranges of Malta. The public criticism by Hay of Fox's methods of training must have been a severe blow to his *amour propre* and as we have seen it caused grave domestic problems. Nevertheless his return to Regimental duties in the capital meant that intellectual life was possible. It was in this period that he lectured on the rifle to the United Service Institution (1858 and 1861), which itself housed one of the largest ethnological collections in the country.

Although Fox has told us that he began his collection at the time he was testing at Woolwich, we have no information at all on it for the first 20 years of its existence. He would have started about the time of the Great Exhibition in 1851, certainly before his marriage in 1853. The anonymous author (Fox) of *Instruction of Musketry* (1854) was very interested in the early history of firearms and probably the collection was confined to firearms for the first few years. At some later date—no doubt after the return from Malta in 1857 but before 1861, when he joined the Ethnological Society of London—it was extended to include ethnological specimens. He had probably already come under the influence of Henry Christy who had a much larger collection with a particular interest in prehistoric antiquities. Christy was one of Fox's sponsors for the Society of Antiquaries in 1863.

We come now to what was the most important change to take place in Fox's ideas during his lifetime. What had been a hobby became a science. The changes in the development of objects that had been his especial interest now, by analogy with biological evolution as enunciated by Darwin, became a new science of cultural evolution and he its chief exponent. The exact steps by which this happened are not recorded. Unlike Lubbock or Huxley, Fox had no formal scientific training and although there must have been immediate interest in the Stanley household in the *Origin of Species* when it was published in 1859, it is unlikely that Fox saw at first any direct relevance to his own interests.

21 Pentre Ifan cromlech: model at Salisbury museum

The realization of the connection perhaps came as we have suggested through Wilde's catalogue of the Collections of the Royal Irish Academy in Dublin. The first two volumes had been published before the *Origin* but probably only became known to Fox when he went to Ireland in 1862. Wilde, a surgeon, was a scientist who had strayed as it were into the field of material culture. If a Linnean classification could be applied to museum exhibits as Wilde tried to do, then of course the study of material culture could be a science. Fox's division of artefacts into classes, sub-classes, varieties and sub-varieties in the late 1860s suggests that is just how he reasoned and that the original idea stemmed from Wilde. If artefacts could be classified on a Linnean system then it was probably a fair assumption that they evolved in a Darwinian manner. Fox's thinking probably had developed in the reverse order—typological development of artefacts resembled evolution and so artefacts must be classifiable like biological species. Wilde had shown him how the two apparently quite unrelated fields of biology and material culture could be brought together.

In Victorian England there was a certain aura about science and scientific attitudes and a certain combativeness of scientists with society, reflecting no doubt in a milder sort of way the much sharper conflict in Roman Catholic countries on the Continent. When Fox returned from Ireland and became Secretary of the Ethnological Society under Huxley the *Origin of Species* had been published less than 10 years.

Huxley was still a crusader leading the forces of science against the hosts of ignorance. In this as in other matters Fox's ideas were certainly moulded by those of the more powerful intellect of Huxley. When therefore Pitt-Rivers tells the Secretary of the Office of Works of the necessity of 'scientific' study of the monuments, or his personal accounts refer to the excavations under 'scientific expenses', one has to remember the overtones that the expression carried. Indeed we shall never understand the motivation behind the Cranborne Chase episode unless we understand the slightly crusading spirit that stirred in the breast of the true scientist.

The boundaries of science were of course a good deal more blurred then than now. Lubbock was a biologist by origin, and a zoologist like Huxley had only been caught up in ethnology because of his interest in physical anthropology. To what extent did scientists in the sense we use the word today really accept Fox as a colleague? It is extremely difficult to say. A number sponsored him for the Royal Society in 1876, of whom the most significant was undoubtedly Darwin who signed the paper from general knowledge. Huxley did not and he may have had reservations on accepting Fox as a true colleague. It is fair to say that he was regarded much more as a scientist then than he would be today.

If the metamorphosis from collector to scientist took place in Ireland his four years at Cork were important for other reasons. For the first time he had responsibility for coastal artillery defences, which no doubt caused him to improve his knowledge of surveying, not normally practised by the ordinary infantry officer. In the Salisbury collection there is part of a textbook on fortification that he possibly required at this period.[1] Six-inch Ordnance Survey sheets, not yet available for southern England, had existed for Ireland for 20 years and thanks to Larcomb antiquities, particularly raths, had been meticulously marked on them. Fox as we have seen counted 10,000 raths in Munster on these maps and the Salisbury papers show that he did a good deal more fieldwork than that published on Roovesmore Fort. Ireland was then troubled by the Fenian disturbances. Fox was involved in these to the extent that in 1866 he acted as prosecuting officer of two senior NCO's charged with Fenian conspiracy and that he had an overall responsibility to keep the authorities informed of the extension of Fenianism, a sort of intelligence task. This caused him to have thoughts on Irish troubles which he regarded as rooted in ethnic and social, not political causes.[2] The thought must cross our minds that the great emphasis he placed on ethnic differences in Cranborne Chase and the significance of the dykes as ethnic divisions owed something to his Irish experiences.

To judge from Fox's draft application[3] the decision to go on half pay and so be free of military duties was his own choice. No doubt he wished to devote his full time to the interests that had emerged while he was at

Cork. Of these two were now clear, cultural evolution and field work (including excavation), while the third, protection of monuments, was embryonic, being limited to awareness of the extent of destruction of raths marked on the Irish maps. Only in the following year or two did plans for protection grow in his mind.

No doubt had Fox been asked in 1870 he would have said the three activities were simply facets of one subject, however they may appear to us. I have treated them in different chapters for it was convenient to discuss them separately, but it must be remembered that they run parallel chronologically, the emphasis being given to this, then that one. It is after all a logical sequence. If you have discovered a key to the unity of human material culture based on a Darwinian model, although not slavishly following it, then your first objective will be to test it and by building up series convince yourself and others that it works. Then you will wish to apply it by digging up monuments from before the period of written records to date them from the material remains within them. The confidence that Fox felt about his ability to date Stonehenge has been mentioned and dating or assigning the site to an identifiable epoch was always one of the main objectives of excavation. This could be done only if one had an intelligible notion of the development of material culture into which to fit the finds. At a certain point the interest of the structures being excavated might replace or supersede the original overriding interest of the theory, especially if there were strongly contrasting remains of different periods present, as in the case of the flint mines and hillfort at Cissbury. I have suggested that the change took place in 1875. For a man with a vision of the unity of human culture, the monuments from the time before written records became documents in their own right, and the need to protect them, was obvious.

The three lectures on *Primitive Warfare* given to the United Services Institution in 1867–69 represent a statement as it were of the origins of human weapons and tools from the imitation of nature up to the age of metal. They are decidedly more Darwinian than the language of Spencer that Fox adopted after 1870, although I am not sure that the thinking altered much. I have suggested that the applied work, such as the 1874 Catalogue or the article on *Early Modes of Navigation*, was more successful than the theory but that perhaps is a matter of opinion.

The vision of Fox has now become a rather mundane standard procedure for dealing with objects of material culture. It is assumed that they did not remain constant but altered and that by moving them around you can ultimately place them in the order in which they were made. This will show some intelligible order of development, their 'typology' to use the word coined by Pitt-Rivers. Where we follow him is in believing that there is a sequence that is rational (usually of improvement) and that it is ascertainable; where most of us do not follow him is in believing that there is some kind of law of nature or natural selection beyond normal human trial and error, controlling this change. The debt of all students of material culture to Pitt-Rivers is immense but few nowadays would share the almost transcendental quality that he attached to typology.

Although his collection went to the branch of the South Kensington museum at Bethnal Green in 1874 and was moved to the main museum in 1878, it must not be supposed that he lost interest in it during the ten years it was in public care. Quite the reverse: from being a fairly small collection he was constantly adding to it so that it was really a different collection when it went to Oxford in 1884. When he was first appointed Inspector his intention was to display his models at South Kensington, not at the Farnham Museum which did not yet exist.[4]

Readers of the Cranborne Chase volumes might be pardoned for thinking that Pitt-Rivers had quietly put aside his earlier views on evolution. This is why his lecture in 1891 with evolution revealed as an instrument of education of the masses through museums comes as such a shock. It would have been in character in the 1860s but in the 1890s it seems an anachronism. The unpublished political papers reveal how evolution—in a rather crude form—was central to his thinking even on everyday matters, right up to his death.

The field-work or excavation of Pitt-Rivers can be divided into three periods: 1864–75, 1875–80, 1880–97. In the first period it was largely a case of foot work: Ireland, the Wolds, the Downs, Thames gravel pits and elsewhere. The excavations were few and not very successful, like Cissbury in 1867 where he failed to recognize the flint mines. His avowed intention was to collect material to build up series comparable to those in his collection. The second period was in Sussex hillforts, commencing with the triumph of Cissbury. The work was financed by learned bodies and he very quickly mastered some of the problems of hillforts. The last period was of course Cranborne Chase, entirely self-financed, on a large scale, lavishly published and with a hint of the official Inspector brooding over the work. There could hardly be a greater contrast in style than that between the second and third periods. There was a switch from hillforts in the second to Romano-British sites in the third, but whether there were new techniques introduced in the third period is open to question. The resources were greater and there was a supporting organisation of trained assistants, so the results were more impressive.

Some points in his experience have been discussed. The great bone deposits found at London Wall in 1866 gave him a permanent interest in the bones of domestic animals; the exposures on the Thames river terraces at Acton in 1869 acquainted him with geological sections. He undertook fieldwork in the Wolds in 1867 while Greenwell was there, although his main debt to the Canon was undoubtedly the knowledge of flint mines derived from the shaft opened at Grimes Graves in 1869–70.

On his return to Cissbury in 1875 Fox knew what to expect.

Had Fox completed the course at Sandhurst we would have unhesitatingly attributed the skill in surveying and sketching that we find in the Inspector's notebooks to the curriculum there, which included both. However he did not do so. He claimed that these skills were largely self-taught and I have suggested that they owed something to military fortification. It is worth recalling that the earliest archaeological surveys of his that we have are from Ireland where he had a responsibility for coastal fortification. Be that as it may, it is to Pitt-Rivers that we are largely indebted for making measured plans and sections the bases of the record of an archaeological excavation. On this three-dimensional skeleton the story of the excavation is fitted like a skin.

Pitt-Rivers was an archaeologist of the chalk in the Wolds, the Downs and in Cranborne Chase, and it was to this particular type of subsoil that his methods were adapted. His characteristic method of tackling an earthwork was to drive a large swath, up to 30 ft wide, through rampart and ditch, the vertical sides of which gave a section or profile of the work. He invented the 'section'—or at least in so far as it was applied to ramparts rather than barrows—which has become the time-honoured method of dealing with earthworks, differing mainly nowadays in the refinement of the sub-divisions within it. In Mount Caburn the extension of the section back into the interior of the hillfort had revealed the characteristic Iron Age pits, and from this of course had arisen the idea of baring large areas of chalk. Sections and baring the chalk were, then, his two main procedures, both of course fairly easily done with paid labourers. The removal of top-soil was a rather crude process in an area that was not divided up into a grid and the whole operation carried out with pick and shovel lacked refinement.

Fairer comparisons are made not with what has followed but with what went before. Here the difficulty is that there is nothing to compare with it. Barrows had been excavated for many years with the burial as the primary objective, and of course Roman villas and towns or foundations generally, but earthworks were regarded as virtually unexcavatable. It is the measure of achievement of Pitt-Rivers that he revealed that useful knowledge could be obtained from these unpromising remains by demonstrating the method required on the one hand and the necessity to study closely the apparently insignificant finds on the other. He had really created modern excavation technique with scarcely any earlier examples to follow. In this as in other achievements it was the ability to start from first principles and create pragmatically something that did not exist before, that arouses our admiration.

The roots of Pitt-Rivers' interest in protection extend back to the evidence on the 6-in. O.S. maps of Munster of the destruction of raths that had taken place, and indeed in which he had himself been implicated at Roovesmore. He was formally involved in the Committee concerned with the protection of megaliths of the International Congress at Norwich in 1868 and was of course very active in this field as Secretary of the Ethnological Society of London in 1868–70. It must have been extremely galling that Lubbock's Bank Holiday Bill went through as quickly as it did, while the Ancient Monuments Bill constantly ran into trouble. He was obliged to be inactive in this decade except for the two practice runs in Brittany in 1878–79 (he spent the intervening winter in France).

Between the period when he received the invitation to become Inspector and the start of his service he was seeking a copy of Viollet-le-Duc's Dictionary with the intention perhaps of deciding how he might emulate the great Inspecteur-General. We have noticed that after his appointment there was a marked change, not so much in the excavations as in their presentation to the world. Contemporaries were of course quick to point out the connection between his official position and his work. Pitt-Rivers did concede '. . . my archaeological establishment, if such it may be called, affords the nearest approach, with the means at my disposal, towards what a Government organisation for archaeological research ought to be . . .'.[5]

We are exceptionally well-informed about the activities of Pitt-Rivers as Inspector, particularly through the survival of the 14 notebooks and sketch-books of himself and his assistants, but also through the official records at Salisbury. How much significance can we attach to his work as Inspector? His function was to persuade owners of monuments named in the schedule to the 1882 Act, or those added by Order in Council, to place them in state care, or 'register' them to use his own expression. The mere reference to a monument in the schedule did not mean that it was 'scheduled' in the modern sense of being protected. The only form of protection was in effect guardianship—that is entering into a deed with the Commissioners of Works for the monument to be in State care. In the 18 years that Pitt-Rivers was Inspector some 43 monuments passed into State care in England, Scotland and Wales; it seems at first sight a pathetic return after all the labours to introduce legislation. After his death no Inspector was appointed until 1910, but in the very changed climate of opinion, the early welfare state, it was possible to introduce compulsory powers in 1913. A foundation had been laid before 1900 and perhaps some of the controversy removed from the subject. It would be unfair to say that an Act without powers meant an Inspector without duties, but the duties of Pitt-Rivers were by general consent light. They did not therefore interfere with the great work in Cranborne Chase; indeed it was surely not an altogether unhappy situation where Pitt-Rivers had the honour and so the stimulus to do the excavations without the burden of duty that would have interfered with them.

In Chapter VII I have discussed the new-found wealth that came to him with the inheritance of the Cranborne Chase estates and the way in which he spent it, apart from the costs of excavation. He seems to have hoped that the Government would relent on its decision not to allow his collection to stay at South Kensington, and only when it was finally moved to Oxford in 1884 did he create the Farnham museum by the conversion of the house that had served as a gypsy school. The precise date is uncertain but it was probably about 1885. The alteration in character of the Larmer Grounds (the erection of a temple in which in 1880 implied more of a park than pleasure ground) caused by the formation of the Rushmore band to play there on Sundays took place at about the same time. The museum of the history of painting in King John's House, Tollard Royal, came slightly later. These and the menagerie of exotic animals at Rushmore were the spectacles to attract visitors. The intention was the same as the modern safari park but the motivation was quite different—educational, rather than commercial.

The introduction of the Indian Houses into the Larmer Grounds seems much more strange to us now than to people at the time of the Diamond Jubilee. It seems extremely odd to start collecting Benin bronzes at the age of 70! They had not, of course, been available before the return of the expedition in 1897 and their first appearance aroused great interest. Some came on the market but many were Government property, some of which Pitt-Rivers apparently acquired through the Crown Agents. It would indeed have been strange if an ethnologist with an interest in primitive art had missed such an opportunity.

The measurements given in the Sandhurst entry show that Fox was tall as a boy and he seems to have been a big man (hence the problems of exploring the galleries at Cissbury!). The earliest photograph[6] shows a figure in a dark coat with fur-lined collar, rather aquiline features and sharp eyes. The portraits and photographs of 20 years later show a stouter figure with a fine head of hair and bushy eyebrows with the same gleaming eyes. In the last years the eyes still gleam out above the heavy beard. It is possible that the prominence of the eyes was heightened by his diabetic condition.

To judge the personality of his subject a biographer's best guides are autograph letters or diaries, but unfortunately in the case of Pitt-Rivers we have few of the former and none of the latter. The only evidence we have, the few remarks of his sister-in-law, Kate Stanley, suggest a moody man, ready to take offence with his wife at the slightest provocation. The difficulties some of his creditors had in recovering their money even when he was a rich man suggest a certain meanness. He was probably not a likeable man, but this after all is true of many who have achieved great things.

I have said something of the religious beliefs of Pitt-Rivers, in so far as they can be gleaned from chance remarks. He did not, like Huxley, delight in announcing his agnosticism and indeed he probably was not an agnostic, for he acknowledged some kind of supernatural authority. I will end by quoting the closing passage from his speech to the Archaeological Institute in Salisbury in 1887.[7] It was intended to be provocative. It represents the views of a man to whom religion was not a central matter and was admissible only so long as it could be reconciled with evolution:

... I cannot myself see how human conduct is likely to be affected disadvantageously by recognizing the humble origin of mankind. If it teaches us to take less pride in our ancestry, and to place more reliance on ourselves, this cannot fail to serve as an additional incentive to industry and respectability. Nor are our relations with the Supreme Power presented to us in an unfavourable light by this discovery, for if man was created originally in the image of God, it is obvious that the very best of us have greatly degenerated. But if on the other hand we recognise that we have sprung from inferior beings, then, there is no cause for anxiety on account of the occasional backsliding observable amongst men, and we are encouraged to hope that with the help of Providence, notwithstanding frequent relapses towards the primitive condition of our remote forefathers, we may continue to improve in the long run as we have done hitherto.

CHRONOLOGICAL TABLE OF THE LIFE OF PITT-RIVERS

This table, which has been compiled from many sources, both in print and in manuscript, will it is hoped be helpful for reference. The blank spaces show how great is our ignorance, especially on the early life of Pitt-Rivers but in later periods as well. The central column shows the year, the left-hand column the place of residence and the right-hand column the main events in his life. Obviously there has had to be a great deal of selection and omission of minor items.

Residing at	Year	Event
Hope Hall, Bramham, Yorkshire	1827	*14 April* Born
	1828	*29 January* Baptized at Sturminster Newton Church, Dorset. *29 July* Bramham Park mansion burnt out.
Bramham Biggin	1829	
	1830	
	1831	
? Move to St James's Square, London	1832	*11 February* death of father at Torquay
	1833	
	1834	
	1835	
	1836	*18 March* elder brother, William Edward, matriculated at Balliol College, Oxford
	1837	
	1838	
	1839	
	1840	
Sandhurst	1841	*19 January* admitted Cadet R.M.C. *29 March* entered 1st Arithmetic and Mathematics class
3 St James's Square		*22 July* retired from Sandhurst
	1842	
	1843	
	1844	

121

(London)	1845	*16 May* commissioned into Grenadier Guards
	1846	
	1847	
	1848	
	1849	First proposal to Alice Stanley refused
	1850	*2 August* Captain
	1851	Involved in testing new rifles at Woolwich ? starts collection
	1852	In France, Belgium and Piedmont studying methods of training in use of rifle. *13 June* death of elder brother in Italy; improved matrimonial prospects
Portsmouth Hythe	1853	*3 February* married Alice Margaret Stanley at St George's, Hanover Square Summer, at Portsmouth with Hay, commandant of new School of Musketry at Hythe Testing at Hythe (Instructor) *19 November* first child, stillborn, to Alice.
Malta Turkey Bulgaria Crimea London	1854	*March*, rifle training in Malta *22 April* embarks on *Golden Fleece* for Scutari *June*, appointed DAQMG to 2nd Division *14 June* Varna *4 September* embarks on *City of London* *14 September* Old Fort, N. of Sevastopol *20 September* Battle of the Alma *c. 30 September* Before Sevastopol *15 October* Leaves Crimea for England *8 November* Arrives London *12 December* Brevet Major
London, Chesham Street Malta	1855	*May* Sails to Malta—rifle training and testing *2 November* first son born in Malta
Malta	1856	Rifle training—Chief Inspector of Musketry in Malta *14 September* second son born in Malta
Malta	1857	*5 May* Lieutenant-Colonel

London		Testing Enfield and Lancaster *August* returns England Criticism by Hay of training methods in Malta
London Park Hill House, Clapham	1858	*9 January* 3rd son born in Brompton Crescent
		June Lecture on rifle to United Services Institution
Park Hill House, Clapham	1859	*27 August* first daughter born (*November*, publication of *Origin of Species*)
	1860	*5 November* 4th son born *December* Alice has nervous breakdown during inquiry into Hay's criticism of Fox's training methods in Malta
	1861	*February* Fox reads Plato *2 December* sails for Canada
Canada Ireland	1862	*11 January* second daughter born while Fox is in Canada *August* appointed Assistant Quartermaster General at Cork of S. District of Ireland
Cork London (1 Chesham St)	1863	3rd daughter born in Cork
Cork London	1864	*Summer* exploring raths and other antiquities near Cork with R. Caulfield *2 June* elected to Antiquaries at same time as Lubbock *17 December* 5th son born in Cork
Cork London 10 Upper Phillimore Gardens, Kensington	1865 1866	Roovesmore Fort in Ireland surveyed *February–March* Prosecuting officer in courts-martial of Darragh and Butler *11 April* 6th son born (last child) *October–November* explores pile structures exposed at London Wall
10 Upper Phillimore Gardens, Kensington	1867	*22 January* Colonel *April* with Greenwell in Wolds *28 June* Lecture on 'Primitive Warfare', I *6 July* to half pay *September* Sussex hillforts and later digging at Cissbury
	1868	*January* digging at Cissbury *April* Fieldwork near Oxford

May T. H. Huxley President of
Ethnological Society
5 June 'Primitive Warfare', II
20–28 August International
Congress of Prehistoric Archaeology
at Norwich and London
(Secretary)
September Fieldwork in Thanet
November Secretary of Ethnological
Society of London

1869   Much of first six months spent
on gravel sections of Thames
terraces above London
18 June 'Primitive Warfare', III
October, digging barrows near
Bangor in N. Wales

1870   *21 June* Emergency meeting of
Ethnological Society about
threat to Dorchester Dykes
27 July attends Greenwell's
lecture on Grimes' Graves

1871   Vice-President of Society of
Antiquaries

1872   *August* British Association for
the Advancement of Science at
Brighton. Excavation of the
Black Berg tumulus

1873   Takes command of W. Surrey
Brigade Depot at Guildford

Uplands, Merrow,   *7 November* death of Mother
Guildford
1874   *1 July* Lecture on Principles
of Classification on occasion
of opening of exhibition of
collection at Bethnal Green
Branch of S. Kensington Museum
Catalogue of part of collection
22 December Lecture on 'Early
Modes of Navigation'

Uplands, Merrow,   1875   *April* Cissbury
Guildford   *28 May* Lecture on 'The Evolution
of Culture' to Royal
Institution
June–September Cissbury

1876   *May* measures men of 2nd
Royal Surrey Militia
2 June Elected to Royal Society

1877   *17–23 July* digging with
Rolleston in Somerset
September–October digging at

		Mount Caburn
		1 October Major-General Gives up command at Guildford
Guildford 30 Sussex Place, Onslow Gardens October:Dinard, Ile et Verlaine	1878	*Summer*–Caesar's Camp, Folkstone, and second campaign at Mount Caburn
		October–November first practice visit on ancient monuments to Brittany
April: 19 Penywern Road, Earl's Court	1879	*March–April* 2nd practice trip to Brittany
		In Scandinavia with Rolleston
		October excavation of Dane's Dyke, Flamborough Head
Rushmore, Wiltshire	1880	Inherits Cranborne Chase Estate and adds Pitt-Rivers to surname
		August—September Barrow-digging at Rushmore with Rolleston
		Creates Larmer grounds and builds round temple in them
Rushmore and 4 Grosvenor Gardens	1881	*March* holiday in Egypt and finds first palaeoliths *in situ* in Nile terraces
		October starts prolonged season at Winklebury Camp which continues until February next year
	1882	*January–February* Winklebury Camp
		1 October Honorary Lieutenant-General
		November invited to be Inspector of Ancient Monuments, post just created in A.M. Act of previous month
		December barrow digging
Rushmore and 4 Grosvenor Gardens	1883	*1 January* takes up duties as Inspector, and begins journeys in Spring
		August addresses Archaeological Institute at Lewes
		29 August starts journey for Scotland
	1884	Inspector's journeys with Tomkin
		June Wales
		August east coast of Scotland
		Pen Pits Report
		October winter season begins

at Woodcuts that continues to
April of 1885
Rushmore Band formed
Collection moved from S.
Kensington to Oxford

1885   *January–April* Woodcuts
27 July left for Scotland with
Tomkin, returning September
October–December, Woodcuts

1886   *30 June* DCL conferred in
Encaenia at Oxford
August–September Carlsbad
4 October begins winter season
at Rotherley that continues to
April of next year

1887   *1 January–30 April*
still at Rotherley
2 August Inaugural address to
Archaeological Institute at
Salisbury
August Derbyshire and South
Yorkshire
October Scotland
First Cranborne Chase Volume

1888   *May–June* begins sections on
Bokerly Dyke
Second Cranborne Chase volume

Rushmore and   1889   Intermittently at work on
4 Grosvenor Gardens   Bokerly Dyke and Woodyates
throughout year
2–17 April Wansdyke
27 July–September Scotland
First use of photography

1890   *20 January–27 February*,
15 April–22 May, Bokerly
Dyke and Woodyates
Builds temple of Vesta at Rushmore
12 June exhibits models of
crosses at Society of
Antiquaries
28 July returns to Wansdyke
This year gives up salary
attached to Inspector's post,
but retains title and office

1891

1892   Seriously ill
July–August Clermont-Ferrand
and Paris
Third Cranborne Chase volume

	1893	*27 April–4 July* South Lodge Camp; *10–24 August* Handley Hill Entrenchment *11 September–25 October* Wor Barrow Ditch
(4 Grosvenor Gardens let)		
Rushmore	1894	*29 March–12 May* Wor Barrow mound
	1895	*April* barrows on Handley Down *5 November* death of youngest son, Arthur Algernon Lane Fox-Pitt *19 November* excavations begin at Martin Down Camp which continue until March of the following year
	1896	*1 January–14 March* still at Martin Down Camp
	1897	*3 August* Presidential Address to Archaeological Institute at Dorchester *September–22 December* excavations at Iwerne
Rushmore		Begins collection of Benin bronzes
	1898	Indian houses at Larmer grounds Fourth Cranborne Chase volume
	1899	
	1900	Catalogue of Benin bronzes *4 May* died at Rushmore; cremated at Woking

NOTES AND REFERENCES

The following abbreviations have been used in the notes:

AJ   *Archaeological Journal*

AL   *Army List*

AP   B. and P. Russell (ed.), *The Amberley Papers, the Letters and Diaries of Lord and Lady Amberley*, 2 vols. (London, 1937).

AR   *Annual Register*

ARCH.   *Archaeologia*

BSF   C. H. Roads, *The British Soldier's Firearm, 1850–64* (London, 1964).

CC   A. H. L. F. Pitt-Rivers, *Excavations in Cranborne Chase*, vols. i–iv (privately printed, 1887–98)

DCRO   Dorset County Record Office.

DNB   Dictionary of National Biography.

EC   J. L. Myres (ed.), *The Evolution of Culture and other Essays by the late Lt. Gen. A. Lane-Fox Pitt-Rivers* (Oxford, 1906).

FI   M. W. Thompson, The First Inspector of Ancient Monuments in the Field, *Journal of the British Archaeological Association*, 3rd Series, xxiii (1960), 103–24.

HBRS   C. F. C. Hawkes, Britons, Romans and Saxons round Salisbury and in Cranborne Chase, Reviewing the Excavations of General Pitt-Rivers, 1881–97, *Archaeological Journal* civ (1947), 27–81.

HGG   Sir F. W. Hamilton, *The Origin and History of the First or Grenadier Guards*, vol. iii (London, 1874).

JAI   *Journal of the Anthropological Institute.*

JESL   *Journal of the Ethnological Society of London.*

LA   Nancy Mitford (ed.), *The Ladies of Alderley, being letters between Maria Josepha, Lady Stanley of Alderley and her daughter-in-law, Henrietta-Maria Stanley*, 1841–50 (London, 1938).

LCA   Leeds City Archives.

RBAAS   *Reports of the British Association for the Advancement of Science.*

SA   Nancy Mitford (ed.), *The Stanleys of Alderley, their letters between the years 1851–65* (London, 1939).

TCS   M. W. Thompson (ed.), *Catalogue of Pitt-Rivers Papers in the Salisbury and South Wiltshire Museum* (forthcoming).

Chapter 1

1. See J. T. Ward, The Saving of a Yorkshire Estate: George Lane Fox and Bramham Park, *Yorks. Arch. Journ.*, xlii (1967), 63–71.
2. HGG, 475.
2a. Certificate of baptism (copy) in possession of Mr. G. A. Pitt-Rivers, the date of christening 29 January 1828.

3. LCA; LF/cviii/24–5; copies of the will of William Augustus Lane Fox describe him as of Bramham Biggin.
4. LCA:LF/lxi/4; J. Foster, *Alumni Oxenienses*, p. 488.
5. AR, 1852.
6. *Complete Guide to the Junior and Senior Departments of the Royal Military College, Sandhurst ... By an Experienced Officer* (London, (1849).
7. I am greatly indebted to Mr G. H. Wright, Deputy Librarian, Central Library, Royal Military Academy, Sandhurst, for this quotation and comments on it in a letter of 27/11/73.

Chapter 2
1. I am grateful to Major P. A. Wright at Regimental Headquarters for this information in a letter of 20/2/1974.
2. HGG, 422.
3. BSF and Fox himself in *Journal of the United Service Institution*, ii (1858) 453–88.
4. HGG, 153.
5. SA, 82.
5a. AR, 1853, 183.
6. LA, 119.
7. LA, 284.
8. SA, 12.
9. SA, 59–60.
10. AP, 121, 280.
11. AP, 13.
12. AP, 121.
13. This suggestion was made to me by Dr C. H. Roads.
14. A. H. Lane Fox, *Catalogue of the Anthropological Collection lent by Col. Lane Fox ...* (London, 1874), p. xiii.
15. DNB.

Chapter 3
1. HGG, 163–4.
2. W. H. Russell, *The Great War with Russia from the Landing at Gallipoli to the death of Lord Raglan* (London, 1855), 2 vols., i, 7–9. These consist of contemporary dispatches to The Times, but his work of 1895 (note 6 below) was reminiscences of 40 years later.
3. BSF.
4. HGG, 166n.
5. HGG. 181.
5a. TCS, A 1.
6. W. H. Russell, *The Great War with Russia, The Invasion of the Crimea, A Personal Retrospect* (London, 1895), 17.
7. Russell (1855), 153; Russell (1895), 16.
8. A. W. Kingslake, *The Invasion of the Crimea*, 3rd ed. (London, 1863), ii, 298–302.
9. Quoted in E. V. Tarle, *Krymskaya Voina* (Moscow, 1941), ii, 22–3.
10. Russell (1895), 66. Casualties in *London Gazette*, 8 October, 1854.

11. Russell (1895), 71ff.
12. The only staff officer of the Second Division to publish letters was D. Lysons, *The Crimean War from First to Last. Letters to his Mother and Sister* (London, 1895).
13. *London Gazette*, 28 September 1854.
14. *ibid.*, 12 December 1854.
15. *Army List* (1874), 51; the certificate of his unfitness for service is in the possession of Mr G. A. Pitt-Rivers. TCS, App. 2, 36.
16. SA, 109.
17. SA, 138.
18. Public Record Office: WO 44/701 C6.
19. SA, 150.
20. SA, 162.
21. SA, 307; H. Busk, *The Rifle and How to Use It* (London, 1859), 84–88.
22. SA, 177.
23. SA, 178.
24. SA, 196.
25. AR.
26. I owe this information to Dr A. J. Taylor who copied it from the Registers of Baptism of the bombed church (which has now been rebuilt).
27. AP, 107–8.
27a. TCS: A, 1c.
28. B. Burgess, *A Brief History of the Royal United Service Institution* (London, 1887).
29. HGG, 319–21.
29a. TCS: A4, 5.
29b. TCS: A8, a–c. The full proceedings of the courts martial are available at the Public Record Office (WO/33/17a, pp. 255–435, 483–91), as well as the doubts and hesitations of the military authorities in these cases (WO/81/113, pp. 119–28 et passim). Thomas Darragh was tried 19 Feb. to 2 March and James Butler 2–8 March, 1866. Both were convicted, Darragh being sentenced to death and Butler to penal servitude for life. Darragh was transported to Australia from which he dramatically escaped in 1876, while in Butler's case the sentence may have been quashed (cf. WO/81/114, p. 11).
30. HGG, 488.
31. LCA; LF/lxi/4.

Chapter 4
1. AP, i, 173. On 25 February 1860 Kate Stanley had been to a lecture by Owen who had warned against too ready belief in Darwin.
2. H. Spencer, *A System of Synthetic Philosophy, The Principles of Sociology* (London, 1874–7), i, 100.
3. Certificate of his candidature at the Society of Antiquaries of London.
4. H. G. Hutchinson, *A Life of Sir John Lubbock, Lord Avebury*, 2 vols. (London, 1914) passim; A. Grant Duff (ed.), *The Life and Work of Lord Avebury*.
5. Hutchinson, 40–42.
6. T. H. Huxley, *Collected Essays*, vii, 155.

7.   *ibid.*, 209–10.
8.   *Transactions of the Third Session of the International Congress of Prehistoric Archaeology* (London, 1869), pp. xvii, 419.
9.   JESL, ns., i (1869), 65.
9a. TCS: A9.
9b. TCS: p. 11, 12.
10. EC; the six lectures were published together but not in the chronological order in which they were delivered, a source of some confusion.
11. EC, 56.
12. EC, 57.
13. EC, 90.
14. EC, 96.
15. EC, 98.
16. EC, 166.
17. EC, 170.
18. EC, 173.
18a. TCS: P, 116.
19. *Catalogue of the Anthropological Collection Lent by Colonel Lane Fox for Exhibition in the Bethnal Green Branch of the South Kensington Museum*, June 1874 (London, 1874, reprinted 1877).
20. JAI, ii (1873), 399–435.
21. EC, 10.
22. EC, 24.
23. EC, 26.
24. I am grateful to the Librarian of the Royal Society for a photostat of this record.
25. *Journal of the Society of Arts*, xl (1892), 115–22.
26. T. H. Huxley, *Collected Essays*, ii, 77.

Chapter 5

1.   Mr C. J. F. McCarthy of Cork has drawn my attention to the work on raths near Cork that he did with R. Caulfield in the summer of 1864: *Gentleman's Magazine*, 1865 (i), 707–10. There are no papers earlier than 1864 at Salisbury so far as I can judge.
1a. *Transactions of the 3rd Session of the International Congress of Prehistoric Archaeology* (London, 1869), 316.
2.   *ibid.*, 317; W. R. Wilde, *A Descriptive Catalogue . . .* i (1857), 100n.
3.   AJ, xxiii (1866), 149; *ibid.* xxiv (1867), 123–39.
4.   *ibid.*, 61; *Anthropological Review*, v, pt. ii (1867), pp. lxxi–lxxxiii.
5.   *ibid.*, p. lxxix.
6.   AJ, xxii (1865), 97–117, 241–64.
6a. TCS: P11, 12.
7.   Although Fox often mentioned having been in Yorkshire in this period his sole reference to being in the company of Greenwell was 12 years later in JAI, xi (1882), 463.
8.   *Archaeologia Aeliana*, 3rd ser., xv (1918), 1–20.
9.   AJ, xxii (1865), 97.
10. *ibid.*, 241.
11. *Arch.* xlii(1) (1869), 27–73.
12. JESL, ns., i (1869), 1–12.

13. AP, 279–80.
14. *Qu. Journ. Geol. Soc.*, xxviii (1872), 449–71.
15. JESL, ns., ii (1869–70), 419–37.
16. *ibid.*, 9 November 1869.
17. *ibid.*, 419–37.
18. RBAAS (1872), 157–74, 187–88.
19. JAI, vi (1877), 280–87.
20. *ibid.*, 443–57.
20a, TCS: P, 40; R, 7.
21. W. Turner (ed.), *Scientific Papers and Addresses by George Rolleston, with a biographical sketch by E. B. Tylor*, (Oxford, 1884).
22. JAI, v (1876), 357–90; TCS: P, 23.
23. *Arch.* xlvi (2) (1881), 423–95.
23a. TCS: P, 28, 29.
24. *Arch.*, xlvii (1883), 429–65.
25. *ibid.*, 434.
26. JAI, viii (1879), 185–91.
27. *Arch.* xlvi (2) (1881), 460.
28. JAI, xi (1882), 455–70.

Chapter 6
1. J. Lubbock, *Prehistoric Times* (London, 1865), 55n.
2. *Transactions of the 3rd Session of the International Congress of Prehistoric Archaeology* (London, 1869), 417.
3. JESL (NS), ii, (1869–70), 412–15, Pl. xxvi; *Proc. Soc. Antiquaries*, v, 92–3.
3a. Mr Stephen Briggs has most kindly supplied me with a photostat of this letter which is in the archives of the 2nd Department of the National Museum at Copenhagen.
4. RBAAS (1872), 172.
5. H. G. Hutchinson, *Life of Sir John Lubbock, Lord Avebury* (London, 1914), 74; A. Grant-Duff (ed.), *The Life and Work of Lord Avebury*, 14.
6. Letter from a 'Late Assistant Quarter Master General' in the *Pall Mall Gazette*, 11/7/1870.
7. FI.
8. G. M. Young, *Victorian England, Portrait of an Age* (London 1953), 41–2.
9. RBAAS (1888), 829.
9a. TCS: B, 483.
10. *Hansard*; TCS: AM, 1a.
10a. FI.
11. RBAAS (1888) 829–33; TCS: AM, 1a.
12. FI. The authorship and arrangement of the books is worked out on pp. 122–24.
13. *Proc. Soc. Ant.*, xiii (1890), 74–81.
14. CC, iii, 245–76.
15. RBAAS (1888), 832.

Chapter 7
1. Will of George, 2nd Lord Rivers in DCRO: D.396/97.

2. *ibid.*
3. These and the following figures come from DCRO: D.396–97 and 98.
4. R. G. Collingwood and J. N. L. Myres, *Roman Britain and the English Settlements*, 2nd ed. (London, 1937), 224.
5. H. M. Colvin (ed.), *A History of the King's Works* (1963), ii, 922–3; *Country Life*, 3 May, 1973, 1218–22; and for the Chase generally W. Smart, *A Chronicle of Cranborne* (1841).
6. DCRO: D.396–98.
7. *ibid.*
8. *Journal of the Society of Arts*, xl (1892), 115–22.
9. *ibid.* 119.
10. *ibid.*, 120.
11. *ibid.*, 117.
12. L. H. Dudley Buxton (ed.), *The Pitt-Rivers Museum, Farnham: General Handbook* (Farnham, 1929) 24–6.
12a. *Proc. Soc. Ant.*, xiii (1890), 74–81.
13. AJ, cv, Supplement (1950), 96–97.
14. *King John's House, Tollard Royal, Wilts* (1890).
15. TCS: M30–37.
16. TCS: L, 1–2, 579.
17. TCS: M39.
18. AP, i, 22.

Chapter 8
1. CC, i, p. xii.
2. TCS: M, 1–23.
3. H. G. Hutchinson, *Life of Sir John Lubbock, Lord Avebury* (London, 1914), i, 109.
4. DCRO: D. 396–98.
5. P. J. Perry, *British Farming in the Great Depression, 1870–1914, An Historical Geography* (Newton Abbot, 1974).
6. *Journ. Soc Arts*, xl (1892), 120.
7. DCRO: D.396/98.
8. RBAAS (1888), 835.
9. Wages in DCRO: D.396/98, but some of the correspondence at Salisbury throws more light on conditions. Peacock was to have a room to himself that was usually shared.
10. CC, iii, p. xvi.
11. HBRS.
12. CC, ii, 233–84.
13. CC, i, 10.
14. Pl. ii in CC, i and Pl. xciv in CC, ii.
15. TCS: P, 84.
16. J. G. D. Clark, *Prehistoric Europe, The Economic Basis* (London, 1952), 117.
17. AJ, xliv (1887), 261–77.
18. CC, iii, 13.
19. There is no need to give repeated references to CC, ii.
20. HBRS, 48–62.
21. *Proceedings of the Prehistoric Society*, ii (1936), 229–30.

22.   TCS: R, 21 and 23.
23.   CC, iv, Pl. 252.
24.   CC, iv, 24–5.
25.   CC, iii, p. 9.
26.   CC, ii, p. xii.
27.   CC, iv, 27.
28.   CC, ii, p. xiii.
29.   CC, iv, 17.

   Conclusion
 1.   TCS: A, 15.
 2.   TCS: A, 8c. 'I arrived at the conclusion that Fenianism must be regarded
       as a war of races indeed'. Cf. AJ, xliv (1887), 261–77.
 3.   TCS: A, 9.
 4.   TCS: AM, 57.
 5.   CC, iii, p. xv.
 6.   SA. plate opposite p. 286.
 7.   AJ, xliv (1887), 276–7.

Appendix One

DESCRIPTION OF THE BATTLE OF THE ALMA

*The following incomplete description of the battle of the Alma is in the posses-
sion of Mr Anthony Pitt-Rivers at Hinton St Mary, Dorset (see TCS, Appendix
2, no 37). It is probably a copy of a description sent home to his wife by Pitt-
Rivers just after the battle on 20 September 1854.*

'. . . of the 1st and 2nd light divisions on our left flank—At last after about half an
hour, the Enemy's Fire began to slacken in one direction and we found that it was
directed upon the left light division which had crossed the river to our left just under a fieldwork which contained a number of heavy guns in position—Our division now advanced across the river and as you may imagine, they assembled in a
regular Mob, on the other side, fortunately there was cover for them to form under—The Guards followed the light division and formed under fire—the 23rd
Fusiliers were driven down into the river and the Centre part of the light Division
were obliged to give way. I saw the Grenadiers advancing in the most perfect line
you ever saw in Hyde Park. They pushed on together with the Coldstream and
Fusiliers, without firing a shot, right under the tremendous Battery of heavy
pieces. The Grenadiers remained firm throughout. They took the redoubt
Battery, capturing one Gun.

The French by this time had captured the heights on our right and opened a fire of artillery across our front. The 2nd Division Batteries advanced on the Bridge and opened upon the retreating Russian Columns. The rout was complete and they retreated across their second line of hills in Complete Confusion.

Just about this time we saw a heavy Column in a ravine on the heights beyond, and for about ten minutes we were doubtful whether they were French or Russians, at last we found they were Russians and began to open our five batteries upon them. Had we done so at first we could have handled them fearfully. The whole then pushed up the heights and the Enemy retreated—we bivouacked that night upon the heights.

Our men behaved manfully and their gallantry is only equalled by their humanity after the battle. I was surprised having heard of men committing all sorts of horrors, to see them just after the excitement of Battle talking so moderately and so attentive to the wounded Russians, who did not understand it—many of the wounded men raised themselves up and shot our men in the backs after they had passed them.

The Russians were reinforced on the field of Battle by some troops who had come into the Crimea during the 5 days we remained near our landing place. They estimate the Russian force at 40 or 50,000. The Russians appear to be well clad and stout men.

A field of Battle is a horrid sight.—I found one spot where every man in the ranks must have been killed, 3 files, apparently by the same ball, lying side by side in the order they stood in the ranks.'

A LANE FOX

ON THE EVOLUTION
OF CULTURE (1875)[1]

If we accept the definition of the term science as 'organized common sense', we necessarily reject the idea of it as a 'great medicine' applicable only to particular subjects and inapplicable to others; and we assume that all those things which call forth the exercise of our common sense are capable of being scientifically dealt with, according as the knowledge which we pretend to have about them is based on evidence in the first place, and in the sequel is applied to the determination of what, for want of a better word, we call general laws.

But in using this term 'law', we do not employ it in the sense of a human law, as a regulating or governing principle of anything, but merely as deduction from observed phenomena. We use it in the sense of a result, rather than a cause of what we observe, or at most we employ it to express the operation of proximate causes; and of the ultimate causes for the phenomena of nature we know nothing at all.

Further, in this development of the principle of common sense it has been said that the inductive sciences pass through three phases, which have been termed the empirical, the classificatory, and the theoretical.

Of these, the first or empirical stage may be defined as representing that particular phase of unorganized common sense in which our knowledge is simply a record of the results of ordinary experience, such as might be acquired by any savage or uneducated person in his dealings with external nature.

But as this condition of knowledge might perhaps be denied the claim to be considered scientific, it might be better perhaps to extend the term so as to embrace all that can be included under a practical knowledge of the subjects treated, in which these subjects are studied for their own sakes, or on account of their practical uses to man, and not with a view to generalizing upon them.

In this way it may be said that agriculture represents the empirical or practical stage of botany; mining, that of geology; hunting and the domestication of animals, that of zoology; the trade of the butcher, that of anatomy; navigation by means of the stars, that of astronomy.

Passing now over the boundary line which separates what are generally recognized as the physical sciences from the science of culture, in which the subjects treated are emanations from the human mind, we find that these also have their corresponding phases of development.

Commencing first with the science of language, which has been the earliest and perhaps the most important branch of human culture the study of which has been scientifically treated as yet, we find that Professor Max Müller, in the series of lectures delivered in this Institution in 1861–3,[2] has shown that the science of language has its corresponding empirical or practical stage, in which it is studied only for its own sake, or for its utility as a means of intercommunication; not as a means of generalizing upon language as a whole, but merely for the purpose of understanding the particular languages which we wish to make use of in our intercourse with others.

In like manner passing from language to the particular department of culture which, for the reasons to be explained hereafter, I shall make the subject of this discourse, viz. the material arts, I shall endeavour to show that there exists also in relation to them a practical or empirical stage, which is the stage that we are now in with respect to them, in which we may include the whole of the constructive arts of mankind, from the simple flint knife to the most complex machine of modern times, when viewed from the standpoint of the mechanic or the artificer, not as subjects for generalization, but merely from an utilitarian point of view.

There are many persons no doubt who regard utility, not as a primary stage, but as the final and highest result of science. But the highest achievements of science, even the highest practical achievements, would never have been reached by the mere utilitarian. There is a force within us by which we are moved in the direction of acquiring knowledge for its own sake and for the sake of truth, regardless of any material advantage to be derived from such knowledge. Sooner or later such knowledge is sure to bear practical fruits, even though we may not live to realize them.

It is in this spirit that men of science have advanced to the second or classificatory stage, in which, with a view to higher generalization, the subjects studied are grouped together according to their affinities, and specific points of resemblance are taken as the representatives of each class.

These classes are at first grouped round independent centres; but such an arrangement of them, having no existence in reality, is purely subjective and can only be transitional. The margins of the classes so formed represent only the margins of our knowledge or our ignorance, as the case may be.

By degrees, as the classes become extended, sub-classes are formed, and they are seen to arrange themselves in the form of branches radiating from a central stem. By further observation, the stems of the several classes are seen to tend towards each other, and we are led to trace them to a point of union.

Thus from the classificatory or comparative we pass gradually into the third stage, which I have spoken of as the theoretical, but which may perhaps be more clearly defined as the evolutionary. By the use of this term 'evolutionary' we make it apparent that our third stage is but a development of the second, evolution being merely the necessary and inevitable result of the extension of classification, implying greater unity and broader generalizations.

These three stages then, the empirical or practical, the classificatory or comparative, and the evolutionary, are applicable to the development of all the inductive sciences.

But it has been held by some that a broad line of demarcation must be drawn between the physical sciences properly so called, such as zoology, botany, and geology, which deal with external nature, and those sciences which have been termed historic, which deal with the works of man.

This question has been ably treated by Professor Max Müller in the series of lectures to which I have referred, a course of lectures which must be regarded as a starting-point and basis of instruction for all who follow after him in the same path.

But in claiming for the science of language, and for language only, a place amongst the physical sciences, he has made admissions to opponents which, in my humble judgement, ought not to be made, and which are inconsistent with that more extended view of the subject by which I contend that, if language, then all that comes under the head of culture must be included amongst the physical sciences. Thus, for example, we find him admitting this passage as a sound and reasonable argument on the part of those who deny the claim of language to be included amongst the physical sciences: 'Physical science,' he says, 'deals with the work of God, historical science with the works of man.'

Now if in dealing with what are here termed the historical sciences, we were to take the subjects of such sciences, as for example the arts or language, implements or words, and were to regard them as entities to be studied apart from their relation to mind, and were to endeavour to deduce from them the laws by which they are related to each other, it is evident that we should be dealing with a matter which could not be correlated with the physical sciences; but such a course would be absurd. It would be as absurd to speak of a boomerang as being derived by inheritance from a waddy, as to speak of a word in Italian being derived by inheritance from a corresponding word in Latin; these words and these implements are but the outward signs or symbols of particular ideas in the mind; and the sequence, if any, which we observe to connect them together, is but the outward sign of the succession of ideas in the brain. It is the mind that we study by means of these symbols.

But of the particular molecular changes or other processes which accompany the evolution of ideas in the mind, we know no more than we do of the particular molecular changes and other processes which accompany the evolution of life in nature, or the changes in chemistry.

If then we are to understand the expression 'the work of God' as implying the direct action of ultimate causes, it is evident that we are not in a position either to affirm or to deny or to make any statement whatever respecting such ultimate causes, which may operate either as directly or as indirectly in the one case as the other. We know nothing about them, and therefore to invoke ultimate causes as a reason for distinguishing between the sciences is to take up a position which cannot be scientifically maintained.

With equal if not greater truth we may combat the assertion that the science of culture is historical, whilst nature, on the other hand, as dealt with by the physical sciences, is incapable of progress. However valid this objection might have appeared during the empirical and comparative stages of the physical sciences, it cannot be maintained, since the researches of Darwin and others have fairly landed them in their evolutionary phase. The principles of variation and natural selection have established a bond of union between the physical and culture sciences which can never be broken. History is but another term for evolution. There are histories and histories, as any one may determine who has read Green's *Short History of the English People*, and compared it with the kind of matter which passed for history in his school days. But our position with regard to culture has always been one which has forced on our comprehension the reality of progress, whilst with respect to the slow progress of external nature, it has been concealed from us, owing to the brief span of human existence and our imperfect records of the past. The distinction, therefore, between the sciences, as historical and non-historical, is but a subjective delusion, and not an objective reality; and herein, I believe, lies the secret of most of those errors that we have to contend with.

But the point in which I venture more particularly to differ from the conclusions of the learned author of the *Science of Language* is the line which he has drawn between language and the other branches of culture by including language amongst the physical sciences whilst he excludes the rest. 'If language,' he says, 'be the work of man in the same sense in which a statue, a temple, a poem, or a law, are properly called works of man, the science of language would have to be classed as an historic science'; and again he says, 'It is the object of these lectures to prove that language is not a work of human art in the same sense as painting, or building, or writing, or printing.'

In dealing with this question it is material, as regards the relative claims of language and the arts to be studied as physical sciences, to distinguish between the general and the particular. If it is said that language as a whole is not a work of human design, the same may with equal truth be said of the arts as a whole. A man who constructs a building, a tool, or a weapon, can no more be said to have devised a scheme of arts, than the introducer of a new word can be said to have invented a language; but each particular word bears the impress of human design as clearly as a weapon or a coin. A word may be said to be a tool for the communication of thought, just as a weapon is an implement of war.

But, says Professor Müller, 'art, science, philosophy, religion, all have a history; language or any other production of nature admits only of growth.' But unless it can be shown that words are entities having the power of generating and producing other words, which arts, tools, or weapons, do not possess, the word growth can only be applied figuratively to language as it is to the arts, and in that case growth and history are synonymous terms. But this is absurd. Words, as I said before, are the outward signs of ideas in the mind, and this is also the case with tools or weapons. Words are ideas expressed by sounds, whilst tools are ideas expressed by hands; and unless it can be shown that there are distinct processes in the mind for language and for the arts they must be classed together.

But it is said, 'language has the property of progressing gradually and irresistibly, and the changes in it are completely beyond the control of the free will of man.' This, however, can only be accepted relatively. We know that in certain phases of savage life the use of particular words may be tabooed in the same manner that the use of particular implements or weapons may be tabooed; but it would be quite as hopeless for any individual to attempt to change the entire course of the constructive arts as to change the form of a language; the action of the individual man is limited in both cases to the production of particular words or particular implements, which take their place like bricks in a building.

Man is not the designer in the sense of an architect, but he is the constructor in the sense of a brickmaker or a bricklayer.

But the difficulty of tracing fleeting words to their sources operates to a great extent in effacing the action of the individual in language. Words become public property before they are incorporated in a language. It would be difficult to establish a system of patents for new words. Here again we see that the line drawn between language and the arts is a subjective delusion, not an objective reality. It is not true that words do not originate with individual men, but merely that we do not perceive it.

Modifications of words, like modifications in the forms of the arts, result from the succession of ideas or other causes affecting particular minds. They obtain acceptance through natural selection by the survival of the fittest.

The chance which a new word or a new implement has of surviving depends on the number of words or implements to be superseded, on their relative importance to the art or the language, and the persistency with which these superseded words or implements are retained. The truth of this is seen in the fact that vocabularies change far more rapidly than grammatical forms; because the same grammatical terminations are employed with a large number of different words, and they are therefore a more constant necessity of speech.

Hence early and barbaric languages may be connected by their grammatical forms long after their vocabularies have entirely changed. The same truth is seen in the fact admitted by philologists, that in small communities new words and modifications of words gain more ready acceptance than in large communities; because the struggle of the new words for existence is less in small than in large communities, and the dialects therefore change more rapidly. And the same causes influence the transformations which take place in the arts. Objects in common use change more slowly than those which are but little employed; the difference is merely one of degree and not of kind.

In dealing with the arts, each separate contrivance occupies a larger share of our attention, to the exclusion of any comprehensive survey of them as a whole. The arts present themselves to our mental vision on a larger scale, and we view them analytically; we are as it were in the brickmaker's yard seeing each brick turned out of hand, whereas in dealing with language we see only the finished building; the details are lost. We view language synthetically. The arts may be said to present themselves to us as a sea beach in detached fragments; language in the form of a compact sandstone. The empiric or the utilitarian may deny that there is any resemblance between them; but the geologist knows that the mode of deposition has been the same in both cases, and he classes the whole as rocks.

Then again there are facilities for collecting and arranging the data for the study of language which do not exist in the case of the arts. Whilst words take seconds to record, hours and days may be spent in the accurate delineation of form. Words cost nothing, may be packed in folios, transmitted by post, and stored on the shelves of every private library. Ten thousand classified words may be carried in the coat pocket without inconvenience, whilst a tenth part of that number of material objects require a museum to contain them, and are accessible only to a few: this is the reason why the arts have never been subjected to those classifications which form the groundwork of a science.

But when we say that words and implements are both tools employed for the expression of thought, it is important to bear in view one difference between them, which has a practical bearing on the relative value of the two studies as a means of tracing the evolution of culture in prehistoric times and amongst savages. The word is the tool of the ear, the implement the tool of the eye; and for this reason language is the science of historic times, whilst the arts constitute the subject of science to be studied in relation to prehistoric times.

Every new tool or weapon formed by the hand of man retains the same form as long as it continues to exist; it may be handed from man to man, from tribe to tribe, from father to son, from one generation to another; or, buried in the soil, it may under special conditions continue for untold ages without change of form, until in our time it may be discovered and employed as evidence of the condition of the arts at the time it was fabricated. Very different, however, is the history of words. Each word coined by the exercise of the inventive faculty of man to express an idea is liable to change as it passes from mouth to ear. Its continued identity is dependent solely on memory, and it is subject to phonetic and acoustic changes from which the forms of the arts are exempt.

When by the invention of writing each word receives its equivalent in forms that are appreciable to the sense of sight, it gains stability, which places it on a footing of equality with the arts, and enables us to trace with certainty the changes it has undergone; and therefore in historic times language is the surest test of social contact that we can have. But in prehistoric times, before it had acquired this permanence through the invention of writing, the forms of language were, to use Mr. Sayce's expression, in a constant state of flux.

The truth of this is seen in the immense number of dialects and languages employed by savages at the present time. Thus amongst the one hundred islands occupied by the Melanesian race, the Bishop of Wellington tells us, and his statement is confirmed by the late lamented Bishop Patteson, that there are no less than two hundred languages, differing so much that the tribes can have but very little interchange of thought; and similar accounts are given of rapid changes of language in Cambodia, Siberia, Central Africa, North, Central, and South America.

The greater stability of the material arts as compared with the fluctuations in the language of a people in a state of primaeval savagery, is well shown by a consideration of the weapons of the Australians, and the names by which they are known in the several parts of that continent. These people, from the simplicity of their arts, afford us the only living examples of what we may presume to have been the characteristics of a primitive people. Their weapons are the same throughout the continent; the shield, the throwing-stick, the spear, the boomerang, and their other weapons differ only in being thicker, broader, flatter, or longer, in different localities; but whether seen on the east or the west coast, each of these classes of weapons is easily recognized by its form and uses. On the other hand, amongst the innumerable languages and dialects spoken by these people, it would appear that almost every tribe has a different name for the same weapon. The narrow parrying-shield, which consists of a piece of wood with a place for the hand in the centre, in South Australia goes by the name of 'heileman', in other parts it is known under the name of 'mulabakka', in Victoria it is 'turnmung', and on the west coast we have 'murukanye' and 'tamarang' for the same implement very slightly modified in size and form. Referring to the comparative table of Australian languages compiled by the Rev. George Taplin, in the first number of the *Journal of the Anthropological Institute* (i, 1872, pp. 84–8), we find the throwing-stick, which on the Murray River is known by the name of 'yova', on the Lower Darling is 'yarrum', in New South Wales it is 'wommurrur', in Victoria 'karrick', on Lake Alexandrina 'taralye', amongst the Adelaide tribes of South Australia it is 'midla', in other parts of South Australia it is called 'ngeweangko', and in King

George's Sound 'miro'.

From these considerations we arrive at the conclusion that in the earliest stages of culture the arts are far more stable than language: whilst the arts are subject only, or chiefly, to those changes which result from growth, language, in addition to those which result from growth, is also affected by changes arising from phonetic decay.

The importance therefore of studying the grammar, so to speak, of the arts becomes apparent, as it is by this means alone that we can trace out the origin and evolution of culture in the earliest times.

The task before us is to follow by means of them the succession of ideas by which the mind of man has developed, from the simple to the complex, and from the homogeneous to the heterogeneous; to work out step by step, by the use of such symbols as the arts afford, that law of contiguity by which the mind has passed from simple cohesion of states of consciousness to the association of ideas, and so on to broader generalizations.

This development has to be considered under the two heads of culture and constitution, that is to say, that we have to consider not only the succession of ideas in the mind resulting from experience, but also the development by inheritance of the internal organism of the mind itself, or, to use the words of Mr. Herbert Spencer, 'In the progress of life at large, as in the progress of the individual, the adjustment of inner tendencies to outer persistencies must begin with the simple and advance to the complex, seeing that, both within and without, complex relations, being made up of simple ones, cannot be established before simple ones have been established' (*Princ. of Psych.*, i³, p. 426).

We find no difficulty in assenting to the general proposition that culture has been a work of progress. Our difficulty lies in realizing the slow stages of its early development, owing to the complexities both of our mental constitution and of the contemporaneous culture from which experience is drawn, or, again to use Mr. Spencer's more expressive words, of our 'inner tendencies', and 'outer persistencies'; we are apt to regard as intuitive, if not congenital, many simple ideas which in early culture can only have been worked out through the exercise of experience and reason during a long course of ages.

We see this error of our own minds constantly displayed in the education of children. The ideas in a child's mind, like those of mankind at large, are necessarily built up in sequence. The instructor makes use of some word, the meaning of which is clearly understood by him, but which does not fall into the sequence of the child's reasoning; the conception associated with it in the child's mind must, however, necessarily conform to such sequence. Hence a confusion of ideas, which is often attributed to the stupidity of the child, but which is in reality due to the inexperience of the instructor; as, for instance, in the case exemplified by Pip, in Dickens' *Great Expectations*, who, having imbibed the precept that he was to 'walk in the same all the days of his life', was led by his sequence of ideas to infer therefrom that he was invariably to walk to school by the same path, and on no account go round by the pastrycook's.

And so in studying savages and early races whose mental development corresponds in some degree to that of children, we have to guard against this automorphism, as Mr. Spencer terms it; that is to say, the tendency to estimate the capacity of others by our own, which appears almost completely to incapacitate some people from dealing with the subject.

The question of the free will of man enters largely into this study. I shall not be expected to say much upon a subject which has so lately occupied the attention of the public, having been discussed by some of our ablest scientists; but I cannot avoid quoting, in reference to this point, a passage from Dr. Carpenter's *Mental Physiology*, who in this controversy is certainly entitled to be regarded as the champion of free will; and therefore by quoting him we run no risk of overstating the case against free will. 'Our mental activity,' he says (p. 25), is 'entirely spontaneous or automatic, being determined by our congenital nervous organism. . . . It may be stated as a fundamental principle that the will can never originate any form of mental activity. . . .' But it has the power, he continues, of selecting any one out of several objects that present themselves either simultaneously or successively before the mental vision, and of so limiting and intensifying the impression which that particular object makes upon the consciousness, that all others shall be for the time non-existent to it.

The truth of this, in so far as regards the limitation of the will, cannot fail to force itself upon the student of culture. It is, I venture to think, by classifying and arranging in evolutionary order the actual facts of the manifestations of mind, as seen in the development of the arts, institutions, and languages of mankind, no less than by comparative anatomy, and far more than by metaphysical speculation, that we shall arrive at a solution of the question, to what extent the mental Ego has been, to use Professor Huxley's expression, a conscious spectator of what has passed.

I propose, therefore, with your permission, to give a few examples, by means of diagrams, of material evolution derived from the earliest phases of culture. In language and in all ideas communicated by word of mouth there is a hiatus between the limits of our knowledge and the origin of culture which can never be bridged over, but we may hold in our hand the first tool ever created by the hand of man.

It has been said that the use of speech is the distinctive quality of man. But how can we know that? We are literally surrounded by brute language. We can imitate their calls, and we find that animals will respond to our imitations of them. But who has ever seen any of the lower animals construct a tool and use it? The conception of man, not as a tool-*using* but as a tool-*making* animal, is clear, defined, and unassailable; probably if we could trace language to its sources, we should be able to draw the same line between natural sounds employed as a medium of communication, and the created word. Thus the arts which we can study may perhaps be taken to illustrate the origin of language, which we cannot study in this phase.

The ape employs both sticks and stones as missiles and as hammers to crack the shells of nuts. But we have no evidence that he ever selects special forms for special uses. The arts therefore afford us a clearly defined starting-point for the commencement of culture.

To go in search of a particular form of stick or stone in order to apply it to a particular use would require greater effort of the will in fixing attention continuously on the matter in hand than is found to exist amongst the lower animals except in cases of instinct, which term I understand to mean an inherited congenital nervous organism which adapts the mind to the ready reception of experience of a particular kind. But this instinct does not exist in the case in question; there is no tool-making instinct: our tool has to be evolved through reason and experience, without the aid of any special organism for the purpose.

The process we have to assume therefore is that, in using stones as hammers, they would occasionally split. In using certain stratified rocks this would occur frequently, and so force itself on the attention of the creature. The creature going on hammering, it would force itself on his notice that the sharp fractured end was doing better work than before. It would be perceived that there were hard things and soft things, that the hard things split the stone, and the soft things were cut by it; and so there would grow up in the mind an association of ideas between striking hard things and splitting, and striking soft things and cutting, and also a sequence by which it would be perceived that the fracture of the stone was a necessary preliminary to the other; and in the course of many generations, during which the internal organism of the mind grew in harmony with this experience, the creature would be led to perform the motions which had been found effectual in splitting the stone before applying it to the purposes for which it was to be used.

Thus we arrive at a state of the arts in which we may suppose man to be able to construct a tool by means of a single blow. By constantly striking in the same direction, flakes would be produced; and by still further repeating the same motions, it would at last be found that by means of many blows a stone could be chipped to an edge or a point so as to form a very efficient tool.

But this continued chipping of the stone in order to produce a tool, implies a considerable mental advance upon the effort of mind necessary to construct a tool with one blow.

It implies continued attention directed by the will to the accomplishment of an object already conceived in the mind, and its subsequent application to another object which must also have been conceived in the mind before the tool was begun.

Now we know from all experience, and from all evolution which we can trace with certainty, that progress moves on in an accelerating ratio, and that the earlier processes take longer than the later ones.

But the implements of the drift, which are the earliest relics of human workmanship as yet recognized, are most of them multiflaked tools, requiring a considerable time to construct, and the use of innumerable blows in order to trim to a point at one end.

It appears therefore evident that in the natural course of events the drift period must have been preceded by an earlier period of considerable extent characterized by the use of single-flaked tools. And we may therefore consider it probable that should any evidences of man be hereafter discovered in miocene beds, they will be associated with such large rude flakes as those now exhibited, which require a feebler effort of attention and of reason to construct.

If we examine the forms of the flint implements of the drift, we find that out of many intermediate shapes we may recognize three in particular, which have been minutely described by Mr. Evans in his valuable work on the stone implements of Britain[3]: (1) a side-tool, consisting of a flint chipped to an edge on one side and having the natural rounded outside of the flint left on the other side, where it appears to have been held in the hand; (2) a tongue-shaped implement chipped to a point at one end, and having the rounded surface for the hand at the big end; and (3) an oval or almond-shaped tool, which is often chipped to an edge all round.

We have no evidence to show which of these kind of tools was the earliest; but that they were employed for different uses there can be little reason to doubt. But have we any evidence to throw light on the way in which these several forms originated in the minds of men in the very low condition of mental development which we may suppose to have existed at the time?

About eight years ago, whilst examining the ancient British camps on the South Downs, I chanced to discover in the camp of Cissbury, near Worthing, a large flint factory of the neolithic age. There were some sixty or more pits from which flints had been obtained from the chalk, and these pits were full of the débris of the flint-workers. The factory was of the neolithic age, the most characteristic tool of which is the flint celt, a form which differs but slightly from the oval or almond-shaped palaeolithic form, but the cutting edge of which is more decidedly at the broad end. The débris, some six hundred or more specimens of which were collected, consisted chiefly of these celts in various stages of manufacture.

If any one will attempt to make a flint celt, as I have done sometimes (and Mr. Evans, from whom I learnt that art, has done frequently), he will find that it is difficult to command the fracture of the flint with certainty; every now and then a large piece will come off, or a flaw will be discovered which spoils the symmetry of the tool, and it has to be thrown away. In arranging and classifying the remains of this flint factory, I found that all the palaeolithic forms were represented by one or other of these unfinished celts, so much so as to make it doubtful whether some of them may not actually have been used like them. A celt finished at the thin end, and abandoned before the cutting edge was completed, represented a tongue-shaped palaeolithic implement; a celt finished only on one side represented a palaeolithic side-tool; and a celt rudely chipped out, and abandoned before receiving its finishing strokes, represented almost exactly an oval palaeolithic tool, only differing from it in being somewhat rougher, and showing evidence of unfinish.

Taking a lesson then from this flint-worker's shop of the later neolithic age, we see how the earlier palaeolithic forms originated. They were not designed outright, as the nineteenth-century man would have designed them for special uses, but arose from a selection of varieties produced accidentally in the process of manufacture. The forms were also suggested by those of the nodules out of which they were made. We see, by examining the outside surfaces that were left on some of them, how a long thin nodule produced a long thin celt, a broad thick nodule a broad thick celt, and so forth. Indeed, so completely does the fabricator appear to have been controlled by the necessities of his art, that in tracing these successive forms one is almost tempted to ask whether the principle of causation lay mostly in the flint or in the flint-worker, so fully do they bear out the statement of Dr. Carpenter and the other physiologists, that nothing originates in the free will of man.

On the two diagrams (22, 23) I have shown how, from the same form of palaeolithic implement already described, the more complex forms of the spear and axe-blade of the subsequent periods were developed. The point developed into a spear, and the broad end into an axe-blade. You will see by reference to Plate I that the oval tool of the drift suggested the smaller leaf-shaped spearhead of the early neolithic age. This, by a gradual straightening of the sides, became the lozenge-shaped form, which latter developed into the barbed form, and this last into the triangular form, which consists of barbs without a tang.

On the other hand, this same oval tool of the drift **23**, when used as an axe-blade with the broad end, became the celt of the neolithic period, chipped only at first and subsequently polished. This gave rise to the copper celt of the same form having convex surfaces, which grew into the bronze celt with flat sides. Then the bronze celt was furnished with a stop to prevent its being pressed too far into the handle by the blow. Others were furnished with projecting flanges to prevent them from swerving by the blow when hafted on a bent stick. Others had both stops and flanges. By degrees the flanges were bent over the stops and over the handle, and then the central portion above the stops, being no longer required, became thinner, and ultimately disappeared, the flanges closed on each other, and by this means the weapon grew into the socket celt. On this socket celt you will see that there is sometimes a semicircular ornamentation on each side. This semicircular ornament, as I pointed out in a paper on primitive warfare read some time ago, is a vestige of the overlapping flange of the earlier forms out of which it grew, which, like the rings on our brass cannon, are survivals of parts formerly serving for special uses.

In the vertical columns I have given, in the order of their occurrence, the successive periods of prehistoric time, viz. the early palaeolithic, late palaeolithic, early neolithic, late neolithic, early bronze, late bronze and iron periods, beneath which I have placed lines for two distinct phases of modern savage culture, viz. the Australian and the American Indian. A cross beneath each form denotes the periods in which they occur, and a vertical bar denotes that they are of rare or doubtful occurrence; so that the sequence of development may be seen at a glance, and it is only a glance that I ask you to take at these diagrams on the present occasion. I have checked them with Mr. Evans' work and also with Sir William Wilde's Catalogue,[4] and I do not think that any

	Side Tool	Tongue Shaped	Oval	Leaf Shaped	Lozenge Shaped	Barbed	Triangular
Early Palaeolithic	+	+	+				
Late Palaeolithic	I	I	I	+	+		
Early Neolithic				+	+		
Late Neolithic				+	+	+	I
Early Bronze				+	+	+	+
Late Bronze				+	+	+	+
Iron Period							
Modern Australian				I			
Modern American				+	+	+	+

+ DENOTES COMMON OCCURRENCE · I DENOTES RARE OR DOUBTFUL

22 Development of the spear

of the statements made in them will be challenged; but as these forms were not developed for the purpose of filling in the spaces in rectangular diagrams, such diagrams only imperfectly convey an idea of the evolution which has taken place, and must be regarded only as provisional and liable to be improved.

In tracing the evolution of prehistoric implements, we are of course limited to such as were constructed of imperishable materials. No doubt our prehistoric ancestors used also implements of wood, but they have long since disappeared; and if we wish to form an idea of what they were, we must turn to those of his nearest congener, the modern savage.

In speaking of savages, the question of progression versus degeneration is probably familiar to most of those present, through the writings of Sir John Lubbock and Mr. E. B. Tylor. To the several weighty arguments in favour of progression given by those writers I will add this one derived from the sequence of ideas. If the Australians, for example, were the degenerate descendants of people in a higher phase of culture, then, as all existing ideas are made up of previous ideas, we must inevitably find amongst their arts traces of the forms of earlier and higher arts, as is the case amongst some of the savages of South America who early came in contact with Peruvian civilization; but the reverse of this is the case: all the forms of the Australian weapons are dirived from those of nature.

In the same way that we saw that the forms of the palaeolithic flint implements were suggested by accidental fractures in the workshop, so the several forms of the Australian wooden implements were suggested by the various forms of the stems and branches out of which they were made. These savages, having only flint tools to work with, cannot saw out their weapons to any form they please; they can only trim the sticks into a serviceable shape. All their weapons are therefore constructed on the grain of the wood, and their

	FLINT					BRONZE					
	SIDE TOOL	TONGUE SHAPED	OVAL	CELT	CONVEX & FLAT SURFACES	STOP	FLANGE	STOP & FLANGE	OVERLAPPING FLANGE	BRONZE SOCKET	IRON SOCKET
EARLY PALÆOLITHIC	+	+	+								
LATE PALÆOLITHIC	▮		▮	▮							
EARLY NEOLITHIC				+							
LATE NEOLITHIC				+							
EARLY BRONZE				▮	+						
LATE BRONZE					+	+	+	+	+	+	
IRON PERIOD											+
AUSTRALIAN			▮	+							
AMERICAN				+	+	+					

+ DENOTES COMMON OCCURRENCE ▮ RARE OR DOUBTFUL

23 Development of the stone and metal axe

forms and uses have arisen from a selection of the natural curves of the sticks.

I have arranged (*see* **24**) drawings of nearly all the weapons used by the Australians, placing them together according to their affinities in such a

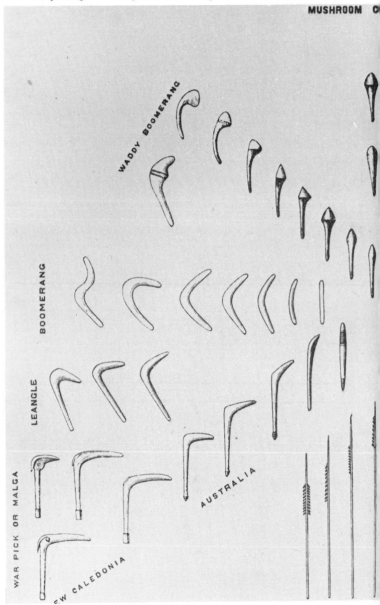

24a, b Derivation of Australian weapons

manner as to show hypothetically their derivation from a single form. As all the forms given on this diagram are drawings of weapons in use at the present time, and there are many intermediate forms not given here, I have not arranged

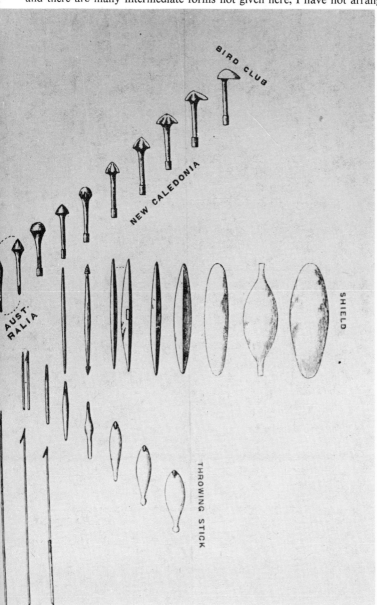

them in horizontal lines, as in the previous diagrams, to show their place in time, but have arranged them as radiating from a central point. We know nothing of the antiquities of savage countries as yet, and therefore cannot trace their evolution in time. The development has therefore been shown by means of survivals of early forms existing at the present time.

In the centre I have placed the simple cylindrical stick, as being the simplest form. By a gradual development of one end I have traced upwards the formation of a sharp ridge and its transition into a kind of mushroom form. To the right upwards I have traced the same development of the mushroom head, the projecting ridge of which is constantly liable to fractures by blows; and as savages always systematize accidental fractures so as to produce symmetry, scollops have been cut out of the ridge in different places for this purpose, which had the effect of concentrating the force of the blow on the projections. These were further developed; one of the pilei of the mushroom head was made larger than the others, and this suggested the form of a bird's head, so that it was only necessary to add a line for the mouth and a couple of eyes to complete the resemblance. To the right we see that the plain stick held in the centre gave the first idea of a defensive weapon, and was used to parry off the darts of the assailant; an aperture was then made in the stick for the hand, and the face of it became broader, developing into a shield, the narrow ends, however, being still retained for parrying. Below I have shown that the long stick simply pointed at one end became a lance; a row of sharp flints were gummed on to one side to produce a cutting edge, and these were then imitated in wood, and by pointing them obliquely they were converted into barbs. To the right another kind of barb was produced by binding on a piece of sharp-pointed wood. Between this and the shields we see that the first idea of the throwing-stick, employed to protect these lances, was simply constructed like the barbed point of the lance itself. The gradual expansion of the stick arose from its being employed like a battledore, to fence off the enemy's lances. To the left below I have shown the gradual development of a peculiar curved weapon, called the 'malga', formed from a stem and the branch projecting from it at different angles. The part where the continuation of the stem was cut off was trimmed to a kind of ridge; this ridge developed, and suggested the crest of a bird's head; ultimately the eyes were added, in the same manner as in the club on the opposite side of the diagram. To the left we see the plain round stick first flattened, then curved. Savages are in the habit of throwing all their weapons at their adversaries and at animals. In throwing a flat curved stick it rotates of its own accord, and as the axis of rotation continues parallel to itself, the thin edge is presented to the resistance of the air in front; this increases the range, and its peculiar flight must have forced itself on the attention of the savage as the result of experience: but he has never had the slightest knowledge of the laws of its flight. The different curves of the boomerang are the natural curves of the sticks, and like all the Australian weapons, they are made on the grain of the wood. Some are thicker than others; some will fly in the curves peculiar to that weapon, and others will not: scarcely two are alike.

To the left above, we see the mushroom-headed 'waddy', with its projecting ridge flattened, then curved; one side becomes more developed than the other, and this being thrown develops into the waddy boomerang, the ridge of the earlier forms being still represented by a mark on the flat head of the weapon;

an intermediate link connects it with the true boomerang.

Many other examples might be given to illustrate the continuity which exists in the development of all savage weapons; but I only ask you to glance at the sequence shown in this diagram and the preceding ones in order to convince you of the truth of the statement which I made at the commencement of this discourse, that although, owing to the complexity of modern contrivances and the larger steps by which we mount the ladder of progress in the material arts, their continuity may be lost sight of, when we come to classify the arts of savages and prehistoric men, the term 'growth' is fully as applicable to them as to the development of the forms of speech, and that there are no grounds, upon the score of continuity, history, or the action of free will, to separate these studies generically as distinct classes of science.

But in dealing with evolution we have to speak not only of growth, but, as in all other natural sciences, of the principle of decay. By decay I do not mean the decay of the materials of the arts, but the decomposition of the mental ideas which produced them.

As complex ideas are built up of simple ones, so there is also a further process by which they become disintegrated, and the parts go to form parts of other ideas.

This decay in the arts corresponds to what is called phonetic decay in language; and in both cases it arises either from incapacity, the desire to save trouble, or the necessity of abbreviating when ideas originally evolved for one purpose come to form parts of other ideas to which they are merely accessory and subordinate, as in the well-known dialect changes of speech. Every sound in language had originally a distinct meaning of its own; gradually these sounds or roots came to form parts of words in which the original meanings of the sounds were lost.

I will now endeavour to draw a parallel to this in the arts, by means of what may be termed realistic degeneration.

I will not say much as to the place of realism in culture. The archaeological world has lately been somewhat startled by the discovery of well-executed designs of elephants and other animals in the French caves in association with the rude stone implements of the palaeolithic age, and by the more recent discovery of Mariette Bey, that the earliest Egyptian sculptures of the third dynasty are the most truthful representations of the human form that are to be found in that country. I see nothing surprising in this, when we consider the power that is developed in many children of eight or nine years old of making drawings of animals and other objects, which, when allowance is made for the feeble hand of childhood, are often as truthful as those of the cave-period men, at a time when their minds have acquired but little power of reasoning or generalizing, or even of taking care of themselves; all which goes to prove that this power of imitation, which is a very different thing from ideal art, is one of the most early developed faculties of the mind of man.

When the power of imitation had once been developed, it would naturally be made use of as a means of intercommunication; thus the drawing of a stag would be made to convey information to people at a distance that there was a herd of deer in the neighbourhood to be hunted; and as the object of the drawing was no longer to depict truthfully the peculiarities of the beast, but merely to convey information, the amount of labour expended upon it would be the least that could be employed for the required purpose. All written characters have originated in this way; and no one now requires to be told how pictographic representations developed into hieroglyphic and subsequently into phonetic characters.

But realistic degeneration would equally take place in all cases in which pictorial representations came to be employed for other purposes than those for which they were originally designed, as in the case of ornamental designs.

So also a coin receives upon its surface the image of a king or a god as a stamp of authority. When from any cause the object of the original design is lost, the object of the stamp being no longer to convey a likeness, but being merely used as a test of genuineness, or perhaps amongst an unlettered people to denote its value, the tendency to realistic degeneration would be proportioned to the difficulties of execution; no further labour would be expended on it than was necessary for the object to be attained. Here I must again remind you of the interesting discourse delivered in this Institution on May 14, 1875, by Mr. Evans, on the evolution of British coins.[5] His examples are figured in his *Coins of the Ancient Britons*, pp. 24–32. You will remember how the coin of Philip of Macedon having been introduced into Britain, the head on the obverse gradually disappeared, leaving only the wreath as a band across the coin, which was ultimately converted into a cross; and how on the reverse, the chariot and two horses dwindled into a single horse, the chariot disappeared, leaving only the wheels, the driver became elevated, not elevated after the manner unfortunately but too common amongst London drivers, but elevated after the manner of the Spiritualists, except that you see he had the precaution to take on a pair of wings, differing also both from the London driver and the Spiritualists, inasmuch as instead of having lost his head he has lost his body, and nothing but the head remains; the body of the horse then gradually disappears, leaving only four lines to denote the legs.

I will now show you an exact parallel to these transformations in a collection of designs, supposed to be tribal marks, which are drawn upon the paddle blades of the New Irelanders, a race of Papuan savages inhabiting an island on the north-east coast of New Guinea.

Having noticed one or two allied varieties of design in specimens that came into my possession, I determined to collect all that I could find as they came to this country. In the course of several years I succeeded in obtaining the series represented upon (**25**).

The first figure you will see clearly represents the head of a Papuan: the hair or wig is stuffed out, and the ears elongated by means of an ear ornament, after the manner of these people; the eyes are represented by two black dots, and the red line of the nose spreads over the forehead. This is the most realistic figure of the series. In the second figure the face is somewhat conventionalized: the line of the nose passes in a coil round the eyes; there is a lozenge pattern on the forehead, representing probably a tattoo mark; the body is represented sitting in full. In the third figure the man is represented sitting sideways, simply by lopping off an arm and a leg on one side. In the fourth figure the legs have disappeared. In the fifth figure the whole body has disappeared. In the sixth figure the nose has expanded at the base, and the sides of the face are made to conform to the line of the nose; the elongated ears are there, but the ear ornament is gone: the nose in this figure is becoming the principal feature. In the seventh

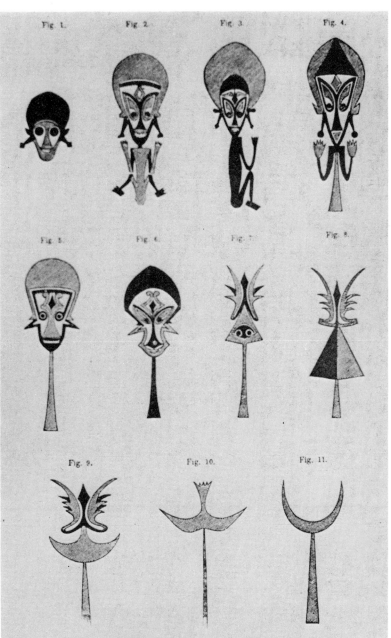

Fig. 1.   Fig. 2.   Fig. 3.   Fig. 4.

Fig. 5.   Fig. 6.   Fig. 7.   Fig. 8.

Fig. 9.   Fig. 10.   Fig. 11.

ORNAMENTATION OF NEW IRELAND PADDLES, SHOWING THE
TRANSITION OF FORM.

figure nothing but the nose is left: the sides of the face and mouth are gone; the ears are drawn along the side of the nose; the head is gone, but the lozenge pattern on the forehead still remains; the coil round the eyes has also disappeared, and is replaced by a kind of leaf form, suggested by the upper lobe of the ear in the previous figures; the eyes are brought down into the nose. In the eighth figure the ears are drawn at right angles to the nose. In the ninth figure the nose has expanded at the base; all the rest is the same as in the last figure. In the tenth figure the lozenge pattern and the ears have disappeared, and a vestige of them only remains, in the form of five points; the base of the nose is still further expanded into a half moon. In the last figure, nothing but a half moon remains. No one who compared this figure with the first of the series, without the explanation afforded by the intermediate links, would believe that it represented the nose of a human face. Unfortunately we do not know as yet the exact meaning of these designs, but when further information is obtained it will throw considerable light on similar transformations in prehistoric times.

My next and last illustration is taken from the relics of Troy, recently brought to light by Dr. Schliemann.[6] In the valuable work lately published by him he gives illustrations of a number of earthenware vases and other objects, called by him idols, having on them the representation of what he conceives to be the face of an owl, and which he believes to represent Athena, the tutelary goddess of Troy, called by Homer 'Glaukopis Athene', which signifies, according to him, 'with the face of an owl.' Professor Max Müller has given his opinion that the word 'glaukopis' cannot possibly be taken to mean owl-faced, but can only mean large- or bright-eyed. On this point I will venture no opinion, but accepting Professor Müller's high authority for the usually received interpretation of it being correct, I shall in no way weaken the evidence in favour of Dr. Schliemann's discovery of the true site of Troy if I succeed in proving that, according to the true principle of realistic degeneration, this figure does not represent an owl but a human face.

The figures on (26) are all taken from Dr. Schliemann's representations, and as the depth of each is given it will be seen that the different varieties of face occur in all the different strata excavated by him except the highest, and therefore no argument as to antiquity can be based upon the depth at which they were found. The two first figures, it will be seen, are clearly intended to represent a human face, all the features being preserved. In the two next figures (3, 4) the mouth has disappeared, but the fact of the principal feature being still a nose and not a beak, is shown by the breadth of the base and also by the representation of the breasts. In the two succeeding figures (5, 6) the nose is narrowed at the base, which gives it the appearance of a beak, but the fact of its being still a human form is still shown by the breasts. Had the idea of an owl been developed through realistic degeneration in these last figures, it would have retained this form, but in the two succeeding figures (7, 8) it will be seen that the nose goes on diminishing.

In the remaining figures, some of which are (12–16) of solid stone, not earthenware, and are believed by Dr. Schliemann to be gods, it is clearly shown by the rude scratches representing the eyebrows, and their want of symmetry, that this degeneration of form is the result of haste.

What then are these solid stone objects? I cannot for a moment doubt, from their resemblance to the vases, from the marks denoting the junction of the

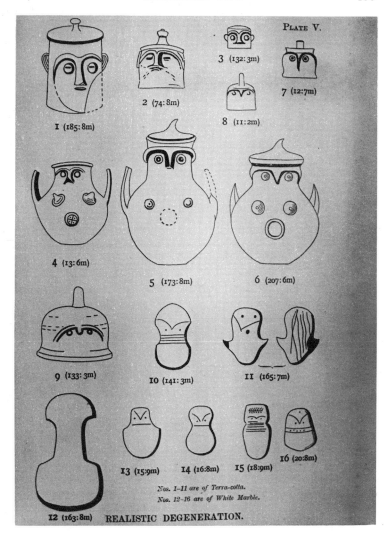

PLATE V.

1 (185:8m)

2 (74:8m)

3 (132:3m)

7 (12:7m)

8 (11:2m)

4 (13:6m)

5 (173:8m)

6 (207:6m)

9 (133:3m)

10 (141:3m)

11 (165:7m)

13 (15:9m)

14 (16:8m)

15 (18:9m)

16 (20:8m)

Nos. 1–11 are of Terra-cotta.
Nos. 12–16 are of White Marble.

12 (163:8m)   REALISTIC DEGENERATION.

26 Representations of the human face found by Dr Schliemann at Troy

cover with the base, and from the representations of handles, that they are votive urns of some kind, similar to those Egyptian stone models of urns represented in the two figures above. Urns of this kind were used by the Egyptians to contain the viscera of the mummies; but with the cheaper form of burial, in which the viscera were retained in the body, stone models of urns, of which these figures are drawings from originals in the British Museum, were deposited in the graves as vestiges of the earlier and more expensive process;

these objects therefore cannot be idols, but votive urns. The fact of human remains having been found in some of the human-headed urns, and the hasty scratches on the stone models, show that they are merely models appertaining to the conventionalized survival of some earlier or more elaborate system of urn burial.

We see from these facts that both growth and decay, the two component elements of evolution, are represented in the study of the material arts.

My object in this discourse has been not, as I fear it may have appeared to you from the brief time at my disposal and my imperfect treatment of the subject, to extol the material arts as being intrinsically of more interest or importance than other branches of culture, but to affirm the principle that it is by studying the psychology of the material arts alone that we can trace human culture to its germs.

The theory of degradation is supported only by the study of those branches of culture of which the early history is lost.

The tree is the type of all evolution: all trees are seedlings, but they differ in their mode of growth. Some, like the beech and oak, throw their branches upwards, and these are typical of the development of the material arts; others, like the straight-stemmed pine, throw off their branches downwards, and these are typical of the development of some other branches of culture. It is quite true, as stated by mythologists, that the history of myths is one of continued degeneration in so far as they can be traced, and that the element of decay enters far more into their composition than that of growth. But the whole accessible history of these myths represents drooping branches from the upward-growing stem of free thought out of which they sprang. What is the space of time which separates us from the Vedas, as compared with the whole upward growth of humanity before and since!

There are huge gaps in our knowledge of the history of the human race, and it has been the pleasure of mankind in all ages to people these gaps with jugglers and bogies; but surely, if slowly, science will open up these desert places, and prove to us that, so far as the finite mind of man can reach, there is nothing but unbroken continuity to be seen in the present and in the past.

---

[1] A Lecture delivered at the Royal Institution of Great Britain on Friday, May 28, 1875, and published in *Proc. Roy. Inst.,* vol. vii. pp. 496–520, Pl. i–iv. This text is based on E.C., pp. 20–44.

[2] *Lectures on the Science of Language* (London, 1861), i, Lecture 1.

[3] John Evans, *The Ancient Stone Implements, Weapons, and Ornaments of Great Britain* (London, 1872[1]), 1897[2], p. 641.

[4] Sir W. Wilde, *Catalogue of the Antiquities of the Museum of the Royal Irish Academy* (Dublin, 1863).

[5] John Evans, 'On the Coinage of the Ancient Britons and Natural Selection,' *Journal of the Royal Institution,* vii, p. 476 ff. This figure has been omitted here.

[6] For illustrations, see *Troy and its Remains,* by Dr. Henry Schliemann (Murray, 1875). The figures may be taken in the following order: No. 185, No. 74, No. 132, No. 13, No. 173, No. 207, No. 12, No. 11, No. 133, No. 141, No. 165. [The figure has been compiled from the references here given.]

INDEX

157